THE CHINESE
BUSINESS PUZZLE

Practical books that inspire

How To Books
3 Newtec Place, Magdalen Road,
Oxford OX4 1RE, United Kingdom
E-mail: info@howtobooks.co.uk
http://www.howtobooks.co.uk

The
Chinese
Business
Puzzle

Andrew M Williamson

howtobooks

Published by How To Books Ltd,
3 Newtec Place, Magdalen Road,
Oxford OX4 1RE. United Kingdom.
Tel: (01865) 793806. Fax: (01865) 248780.
email: info@howtobooks.co.uk
http://www.howtobooks.co.uk

British Library Cataloguing in Publication Data
A catalogue record for this book is available from the British Library

Cover design by Baseline Arts Ltd, Oxford
Produced for How To Books by Deer Park Productions
Typeset by PDQ Typesetting, Newcastle-under-Lyme, Staffs.
Printed and bound in Great Britain by Cromwell Press Ltd, Trowbridge, Wiltshire

NOTE: The material contained in this book is set out in good faith for general
guidance and no liability can be accepted for loss or expense incurred as a result of
relying in particular circumstances on statements made in the book. The laws and
regulations are complex and liable to change, and readers should check the current
position with the relevant authorities before making personal arrangements.

ISBN: 1 85703 882 7

Contents

About the Author

Andrew Williamson (born 1945) is a scholar of Repton and graduate of Bristol, where he studied modern languages.

At the same time, he developed a lifelong interest in classical choral music, which he was fortunate to be able to combine with his degree – in particular reading music at the Sorbonne and directing a student choir at Heidelberg University (courtesy of a German Government scholarship).

Whilst at Bristol, he met his wife, Eileen, also a musically-gifted modern language student, whom he married in July 1969, and with whom he has continued to 'make music' ever since.

Keen to travel, Andrew joined a major international insurance company and subsequently spent 12 of his 30-years career overseas in three continents – Europe (Spain and Italy), South America (Colombia) and Asia (China) – whilst Eileen taught English, primarily with the British Council.

Whilst abroad, they always became fully involved in the local and expatriate communities – for example, Andrew was elected in:

◆ **Spain**: president of the local property owners' association on several occasions by his all-Spanish neighbours

◆ **China**: to the Committee of the British Chamber of Commerce in China by the British business community.

Two of their sons were born and initially educated abroad, speaking Spanish before English; whilst Number Three first saw light of day in England, and had to contend with spending school holidays in China.

Andrew held some very senior appointments with his employer abroad (e.g. General Manager for Colombia) and at home (e.g. Distance Learning Manager) before being appointed Director and Chief Representative for China in the late 1990s – with the brief to direct the company's China Market Entry Team

In China, Andrew was involved amongst other things with:

- raising the **company's profile and influence** in China-based Chinese and British government, diplomatic and business circles

- establishing a 'circle of friends' from which to select a **joint venture** partner

- **market intelligence**.

In recognition of his services, the People's Bank of China appointed Andrew a guest professor of its Shanghai Finance College.

As a result, Andrew has first-hand, in-depth and relevant practical expertise in and experience of:

- **in general**: the cross-cultural challenges that face inexperienced and seasoned foreign business(wo)-men working in established and emerging markets; and sadly witnessed many failed ventures due to insufficient attention being paid by employers to their employees' cross-cultural needs

- **in particular**: the issues facing foreigners who wish to work with the Chinese, including building a business presence in China virtually from scratch.

Consequently, now retired, he and Eileen act as freelance China consultants to Farnham Castle, briefing foreign business people and their spouses on working with the Chinese and living in China; and spend their spare time exploring the English waterways on their aptly named cruiser *Guanxi*, and entertaining their grandchildren.

Further information: www.minim.biz

Abbreviations

The following standard English abbreviations are used in this book.

The first time that each one appears, the full meaning is given. Thereafter, only the abbreviation is used.

Abbreviation	Meaning
AD	Anno Domini
aka	also known as
am	in the morning
BC	Before Christ
c.	circa/approximately
CCPIT	China Council for the Promotion of International Trade
CD	compact disk
CEO	chief executive officer
CIA	Central Intelligence Agency
CII	Chartered Insurance Institute
CIPD	Chartered Institute of Personnel and Development
CPAA	Chinese Performing Arts Agency
CPC	Communist Party of China
CPI	Consumer Price Index
CSRC	China Securities Regulatory Commission
DG	director general
ed.	edition
e.g.	for example
EU	Evaluated Unit
FAQ	frequently asked question
FDI	foreign direct investment
FESCO	Foreign Enterprise Service Corporation
GDP	gross domestic product
GM	general manager
HK(SAR)	Hong Kong (Special Administrative Region)
HR(M)	human resource (management)
HSBC	Hong Kong and Shanghai Banking Corporation
ibid	previously quoted source
i.e.	that is
IiP	Investors in People
IPR	Intellectual Property Rights

IT	information technology
JE	job evaluation
JV	joint venture
KPI	key performance indicator
M/As	Mergers and Acquisitions
MBA	Master of Business Administration
MOFTEC	Ministry of Foreign Trade and Economic Co-operation
MOU	Memorandum of Understanding
MSG	monosodium glutamate
No	number
NPL	Non Performing Loan
NT	Royal National Theatre
op. cit	previously quoted source
p.a.	per year
PA	personal assistant
PBOC	People's Bank of China
PICC	People's Insurance Company of China
pm	in the afternoon/evening
PLA	People's Liberation Army
POE	Privately Owned Enterprise
p(p).	page(s)
PR	public relations
PRC	People's Republic of China
PSB	Public Security Bureau
RMB	Renminbi
SDPC	State Development Planning Commission
SETC	State Economic and Trade Commission
SEZ	Special Economic Zone
sic	as written in the original
SIETAR	Society for Intercultural Education, Training and Research
SOE	State Owned Enterprise
TV	television
UK	United Kingdom
UN	United Nations
US(A)	United States (of America)
US$	US dollars
VIP	very important person
WOFE	wholly owned foreign enterprise
WTO	World Trade Organisation

Farnham Castle International Briefing and Conference Centre

A lack of cultural understanding and local practices can be a major obstacle to the effectiveness of conducting business in another country. The ability to relate quickly and effectively with colleagues and clients in a new country is very important to long-term success.

Farnham Castle International Briefing and Conference Centre is widely acknowledged as the world's leading provider of intercultural management training and briefing and has an unmatched reputation for helping individuals, partners and their families to prepare to live and work effectively anywhere in the world.

Through its unrivalled faculty of trainers and experts, Farnham Castle offers a totally flexible and comprehensive range of programmes providing the first-hand knowledge and skills required to be successful in international business including –

♦ workshops on developing cross cultural awareness

♦ working effectively with specific cultures or nationalities

♦ cross cultural communication, presentation and negotiation skills training

♦ country and business briefings for any country in the world

♦ intensive tuition in any language.

So before you go anywhere else, make sure you visit Farnham Castle because books are never enough!

Full details available on web site at: www.farnhamcastle.com

Foreword

The past 25 years of reform in China have been remarkable and the Chinese Communist Party knows that to retain the monopoly of political power, it must improve the lot of the Chinese people and raise standards of living. During that time, it has walked a political tightrope, balancing the short-term pain of economic reform against the longer-term benefits of building successful companies that can compete in world markets and generate the wealth required to yield the rising living standards that justify its leading role.

Under Premier Zhu Rongji (1998–2003), foreign trade grew, Foreign Direct Investment overtook the USA to top the FDI league table, and government expenditure increased, enabling China to sustain growth rates of around 8 per cent – a remarkable achievement against a background of successive international economic shocks from the 'Asian crisis' of 1997, to the recent stock market crashes. When in March 2003, therefore, China completed the first smooth transition of political power in 53 years, her political and economic outlook seemed bright.

Then came Severe Acute Respiratory Syndrome (SARS) – whose full effect will depend on the government's success in combating the disease, against which the authoritarian nature of the Party's rule may permit the use of draconian measures unacceptable in democratic countries. Meanwhile, the pundits who were previously confident that China's GDP growth estimate for 2003 of 7 per cent was less than ambitious are now talking of 5 per cent or lower.

The combination of slower growth and the sense that government secrecy and a muzzled press contributed to the spread of SARS may be a dangerous political cocktail. It is generally believed that China requires growth of 5 per cent per annum just to absorb the annual increase in the working population and maintain living standards. The unusually frank acknowledgement that mistakes were made in handling SARS, and the dismissal of senior officials, indicates that the Party and government recognise the threat.

SARS aside, the leadership recognises the importance of foreign trade and investment in revitalising the Chinese economy and preserving the

Party's rule; and of the private sector in building China's economic strength. At the November 2002 Congress, the Party amended its constitution to include people from the burgeoning private business sector alongside the workers, peasants and soldiers of Party tradition. This followed an earlier amendment to the state constitution giving equal protection to private business under the law, alongside state-owned and collective enterprises, the old mainstays of the socialist economy.

The stage is now set for the private sector to become an ever more important driver of the Chinese economy and possibly the saviour of the Party itself.

A capitalist economy is one thing; a bourgeois republic another. The Party is determined to defend its leading role and resist calls for a multi-party system, insisting on the principle of 'democratic central-ism'. Beware those who tell you that China is now a market economy! The role of the Party and government in business is still all-pervading, even if the mechanisms for micro-economic management are being dismantled. For now, liberal economics are a long way off, and there is little doubt that a residual power remains to intervene at will.

Separation of government from business is critical to creating the level playing field on which all enterprises can compete equally and is needed to guarantee 'national treatment' for foreign traders and investors – a sacrosanct commitment that China undertook in joining the World Trade Organisation. The Party, whose leading role is mandated by the state constitution, is set on this course, believing it necessary to deliver economic development.

At the same time, the Party's representation within enterprises is one of the most important social control mechanisms which it is reluctant to relinquish, despite widespread acknowledgement of its deleterious economic consequences. Thus, there is continuous tension between the objective of resting the Party's claim to legitimacy on increased prosperity and its desire to retain the tried and tested methods of social management as a safeguard against social unrest.

Attempts to reconcile these incompatible factors have spawned countless inconclusive reforms intended to rationalise the system of ownership, exercise of ownership rights, regulation, management and supervision. The reforms announced at the March 2003 National People's Congress were yet another attempt to streamline the system and reconcile the irreconcilable...and inevitably flawed.

Other challenges facing the new leadership include reforming loss-making state-owned enterprises; rescuing banks from the burden of non-performing loans; curbing corruption; establishing and funding a social security system; building effective and trustworthy systems to invest the Chinese people's enormous pool of savings...the list goes on.

Remarkably, the Chinese political apparatus continues to grapple with these issues and is so well on the way to achieving a revitalised manufacturing sector that Western commentators are dubbing China 'the workshop of the world'. China also seeks foreign capital, equipment, technology, know-how and management expertise to help in solving its problems and is prepared for foreign investors and traders to earn a decent return in exchange; and is continuously improving the environment for foreign investors because it recognises that it needs and will continue to need them.

Thus, the challenges that China faces present an enormous opportunity for foreign businessmen that will grow in the years and decades ahead. The key to success in China is to do your homework carefully and to apply normal business principles in the light of a good understanding of the environment in which you are operating.

That is what this book will help you to do. It gives the reader, in concise form, an understanding of the environment in the widest sense, including the history, the culture, the beliefs, the mind-set, the etiquette and the business practices. With it you will be well equipped to set out to tackle the China Market, which has fascinated, frustrated, beguiled – and sometimes enriched – Western businessmen for almost two centuries.

Peter Batey OBE
Chairman, Apco Batey Burn
Beijing, May 2003

Introduction

> They also serve who only stand and wait.
> *On his blindness*, John Milton

There is no straightforward formula for foreigners to succeed in doing business with the Chinese. Pretending otherwise risks failure. Thus, each old China-hand will advise green-horns differently, according to their personal experience of what works or not. However, such advice does not, but should, come with the health warning that 'one man's meat is another man's poison'. So:

♦ Lesson 1: seek a second opinion, then a third from a Chinese person, and finally a fourth from someone who really knows, understands and is respected by both sides.

♦ Lesson 2: beware of self-styled China 'experts' or 'consultants'.

To quote a joke doing the rounds in China a few years ago:

Question: What is the difference between a China 'expert' and a China 'consultant'?

Answer: An expert is anyone who has been in China for 30 minutes; a consultant is someone who knows more about China than you do.

I claim to be neither. However, during my time in China I met many who did; and I was privileged to befriend a handful who really are, both foreign and Chinese, who took the time and trouble to share their expertise with me. To them, I acknowledge my debt of gratitude and dedicate this book; and in particular my Chinese ex-colleagues: Vivian Xu (bi-lingual Personal Assistant) and John Shen (Chief Representative, Shanghai) – both of whom figure prominently in the book – for all their assistance, especially during our visit to Shanghai in February 2003.

Origin

The motivation behind this book is twofold – to:

1. Pass on my passion for and experiences of China and the Chinese to others, in the hope that they will catch the vision and learn from my mistakes.

2. Thank my wife, Eileen, without whose altruistic support and encouragement such experiences, let alone this book, would have been impossible.

It all started on Boxing Day 1996, when I casually asked Eileen, just as I was slipping out of the cottage into the garden (as husbands do, when they are not sure how violent the reaction is going to be!): 'There's a vacancy in China ... how do you fancy going?' – and she replied: 'Yes!' Our family was astounded: all that any of us knew about China was from the film *The Inn of the Sixth Happiness* and a biography of Gladys Aylward that I had read some 40 years earlier. The rest, as they say, is history.

Credentials

Although we returned to England less than two years later, our training as linguists and previous expatriate experience (mentioned elsewhere) greatly accelerated our learning curve whilst in China. Also, the intensive nature of my work (obtaining an operating licence) rapidly and constantly exposed me to the key issues of working with senior Chinese officials. Subsequently, we have maintained our momentum through continuing study in support of our work on behalf of Farnham Castle International Briefing and Conference Centre (UK), which has in turn given birth to this book.

Authenticity and confidentiality

An erstwhile boss (and friend) of mine once said that mistakes are learning opportunities; for which reason this book 'tells it as it is', warts and all, not only suggesting and illustrating best practice but also quoting my own 'learning opportunities'.

To protect the third parties involved, and respect the confidentiality of my employer (of which I am now a pensioner), I have anonymised some examples quoted where and as appropriate. Nevertheless, all such illustrations are wholly genuine; and suggestions based on hard fact.

Target audience

The book is aimed at foreigners who wish to do business with the

Chinese, whether in China or at home, face-to-face or at a distance, during a long-term posting or on a flying visit.

Whilst not specifically written for Westerners, my own background (traditional privileged English middle-class education), beliefs (Evangelical Anglican), business career (Europe and South America), management style (coach-facilitator) and behavioural preferences (extraversion, intuition, feeling and judging) may inevitably creep in from time to time – so you have been warned!

Structure and contents

Like Caesar's Gaul, the book is divided into three parts:

Part	Description
1.	Overview of the Chinese business and social environments, and underpinning behaviours
2.	Detailed examination of the Chinese business principles and practices
3.	Detailed consideration of the human resouce management issues in China

The content of the chapters is cumulative – that is: each one develops earlier ones and is developed by later ones. Thus, each chapter:

◆ starts – except for the first – with a table of the corresponding preceding underpinning knowledge

◆ finishes – except for the last – with a table of the corresponding subsequent application.

In particular, as a direct consequence of the many and varied 'how to' questions at our briefings at Farnham Castle, mentioned above, I have organised much of the material into stand-alone lists and tables of guidelines for specific subjects, supported by real examples and case studies. In this way, I hope that readers can quickly find specific answers to specific questions, grouped by topic, without having to plough through masses of prose.

Such guidelines apply irrespective of where in the world, since most Chinese prefer to do business their way, even outside China – perhaps because they may consider themselves less well-travelled than their foreign counterparts who, consequently, are probably able more easily to adapt to other cultures (and cuisines), even in their home country.

Terminology

By the terms 'Chinese' and 'China', I specifically mean the people, Provinces and Municipalities of the People's Republic of China in general, and the major centres of industry and commerce in particular.

While the Special Administrative Regions (Hong Kong and Macau), Autonomous National Minority Areas (Guangxi, Inner Mongolia, Ningxia, Tibet and Xinjiang) and Province of Taiwan (also known as the Republic of China) undoubtedly have close similarities, China is such a large, diverse and quickly evolving country that it would be imprudent of me to make such bold assumptions.

Because of her size, however, there is a danger in adopting an identical approach to all Chinese in every part of China and/or elsewhere – when, in fact, they are as diverse as the many nationalities that make up Europe; and their regional loyalties rival each other just as fiercely as between the supporters of the White and Red Roses in England!

I have, therefore, tried to reflect the eternal truths of China and her culture; but apologise in advance for overlooking any significant regional or ethnic variations.

Disclaimer

Indeed, the pace of change in China, in all walks of life, moves so fast that what was unheard of yesterday and is news today may be out-of-date tomorrow.

Consequently, this book is obsolete even as I write it – for which reason it should be used as an illustrative (rather than exhaustive) good-practice guide to be supplemented by your own more recent experience and research. To guard against future inaccuracies – for which it would be unfair to hold me liable in such circumstances – you should, therefore, always seek up-to-date advice if in doubt.

Meanwhile, I have tried to reflect the most obvious relevant outcomes, actual and likely, of the recent 16th Communist Party of China

National Congress of November 2002 and the 10th National People's Congress of March 2003.

Health warning

Although my wife and I are graduate linguists, had previously worked abroad for ten years (mentioned elsewhere) – during which time we raised a young family – and my employer insisted that we both visit China before accepting the appointment, no amount of prior instruction could have adequately prepared us for what lay in store, despite our own and others' best efforts.

Hopefully this book will help you unravel the puzzle that is China; but it is no substitute for the real thing. Enjoy working with the Chinese ... they are well worth the effort!

Objectivity

> *Judge not, that ye be not judged*
> [Matthew, 7.1]

Judging foreign cultures by your own standards is an arrogant disregard for, and ignorance of, others' ways of life, fraught with dangers; and China is no exception.

EXAMPLE

Whilst writing and researching this book, I was privy to a fallacious argument condemning the defunct Chinese practice of binding women's feet – when my retort that, at the same time in England children were being sent up chimneys, was met with howls of protest!

Thus, if you wish to work effectively with the Chinese, the more you understand and respect their culture – without either condemning or accepting it – the more successful you are likely to be.

By the same token, this book tries to be as objective as possible, describing what happens and explaining why, but without knowingly justifying or condemning Chinese practice. For maximum benefit, therefore, please treat it as such.

Postscript

Do not underestimate the Chinese... we still have much to learn from them!

Andrew M. Williamson
BA, FCII, FCIPD, DipCMus
Chartered Insurance Practitioner
Guest Professor, Shanghai Finance College
Managing Partner, Minim Consulting
East Anglia, 9th May 2003

1
Business Environment

This Chapter presents an overview of the relevant background to the business environment in which foreigners may expect and be expected to work with the Chinese, whether at home or in China. It is divided under five headings:

1. The logical starting point is the **philosophical environment** of **Confucianism** – which, albeit out of favour at present, has so permeated Chinese life for the last 2,500 years that its effect is subconsciously all-present, including in business. (See also: Appendices 1.1 and 1.2.)

2. Next is the **political environment** that has marginalised Confucianism to dominate China since 1949: communism – which has evolved into '**socialism with Chinese characteristics**'.

3. Integral to her political environment is China's **economic environment** – where 'socialism with Chinese characteristics' translates into a '**market economy with Chinese characteristics**'.

4. A key aspect of that economy is China's '**open door policy**', which directly impacts on the opportunities for foreign business.

5. Last but not least is the **legal environment** – that legislates how business should operate within the preceding four environments.

Chapter 2 is complementary, dealing with the corresponding social environment.

Both chapters give a sufficient underpinning knowledge to allow a better understanding and, consequently, practical implementation of the 'how to do what' more effectively when working with the Chinese.

PHILOSOPHICAL ENVIRONMENT

Although China is officially an atheist country without any scriptures that are formally recognised in the traditional sense, there is no doubt that the Chinese way of life is a legacy of Confucianism.

Confucianism

Confucianism is a form of humanism, based on the teachings of Confucius. Although once elevated to the status of China's official state ideology, it has never become an established religion. This is due to the primarily secular nature of its philosophy, and Confucius not having sought or claimed divinity.

Since the collapse of the Chinese Empire (1911) in general, and the founding of the People's Republic of China (PRC) (1949) in particular, Confucianism has fallen from grace and no longer dominates Chinese political life and institutions.

Nevertheless, some Chinese scholars suggest that Confucian virtues and values – handed down from generation to generation as memorable common-sense practical sayings, aphorisms and anecdotes – will remain the bedrock of Chinese ethics.

If so, then such practices will apply equally to business dealings. Therefore a basic understanding of them by non-Chinese can only improve their working relationships with the Chinese.

Rise and fall of Confucianism

Confucius lived from 551 to 479 BC.

His teachings alternated between periods of:

♦ unrivalled pre-eminence as the state orthodoxy of the **Han**, **Tang** and **Qing dynasties**

♦ strong competition from **Taoism** and **Buddhism**

re-emerging each time stronger than before, until finally ceding in the twentieth century first to Western influences and then (as now) **communism**.

Origins of Confucianism

Rather than invent Confucianism, Confucius revitalised and passed on the earlier canon of the Age of the Grand Harmony that the way to achieve social cohesion is by ritual observance, not legal constraint, as a communal act to promote mutual understanding.

Generally: he advocated the principles of good conduct, practical wisdom and proper social relationships that, for countless generations of Chinese since, have:

◆ influenced the attitudes to life
◆ set the models of behaviour and social values
◆ set the standards for training government officials
◆ laid the foundation for political theories and institutions.

Explicitly: he espoused the following key concepts on which such principles were built:

Key concepts of Confucianism	
Concept	**Meaning**
lì	self-benefit (avoidance of)
lǐ	propriety, ritual, respect for others
rén	benevolence, love for others
shù	reciprocity
xiào	love of children for parents and vice-versa, filial piety
yì	righteousness, uprightness
zhōng	sincerity, faithfulness to oneself and others

Golden Rule of Confucianism

The first concept is a warning; the rest, values at the heart of which is '*rén*' manifested by '*zhōng*' and '*shù*'. Indeed, when asked to summarise his teaching in one word, Confucius replied '*shù*' or **'reciprocity'**, expressed as 'What you do not want done to yourself, do not do to others' *(Analects* 15:23).

This is Confucius' **Golden Rule**; and, rather than being interpreted purely as a prohibition, should be construed also as a negative command intended to encourage a positive outcome: 'The man of perfect virtue, wishing to be established himself, seeks also to establish others; wishing to be enlarged himself, he seeks also to enlarge others' (*Analects* 6:30).

Filial piety

Another key concept of Confucianism is **filial piety** (the respect of children for their parents, and vice-versa), expressed as: 'In serving his parents, a son may remonstrate with them, but gently; when he sees that they do not incline to follow his advice, he shows an increased degree of reverence, but does not abandon his purpose; and should they punish him, he does not allow himself to murmur' (*Analects* 4:18).

Motivated by a recognition of and reverence for the source of life – rather than blind obedience to parental authority – *xiào* should be construed as a unilateral command intended to encourage a bilateral outcome of mutual respect that encourages both parents and children to flourish. For example: if a father fails to behave properly, asks Confucius, how can he expect his son to follow ritual?

It follows that:

◆ If:
   – such conduct engenders familial harmony, and
   – families are the basic unit of society; or
   – conversely, society is just an extended family

◆ then:
   – the same conduct should similarly engender nationwide political stability and social order through the tiers of school, local community, province etc; and
   – translate into other relationships such as: ruler–subject, master–servant, husband–wife, teacher–pupil, old–young, friend–friend etc.

Thus, as regards:

◆ *politics*: Confucius advocated a paternalistic and strictly hierarchical government:

  – with a benevolent, honourable ruler; and respectful, obedient subjects
  – where the former sets an example to the latter by preferring doing good to personal gain or force
  – that provides food, security and education for the people.

♦ *business*: the same concepts apply to such working relationships as employer–employee, supplier–customer, joint venture partners, licensor–licensee.

Western parallels

It should not be too difficult for Western business people to understand and emulate the foregoing concepts, as they are mirrored in Judeo-Christian theology and the teachings of St Paul quoted in the following table:

Confucian concept	Judeo-Christian theology	Teachings of St Paul
benevolence and reciprocity	love your neighbour as yourself	charity (2 Cor 13)
filial piety and mutual respect	honour your father and your mother	Christian household (Eph 5:21–6:9)
personal gain	the love of money is the root of all evils	(1 Tim 6:10)

The Superior Man

That Confucius laid great store by correct behaviour is underlined by his devoting the whole of Chapter 10 of the *Analects* to specific rituals for specific occasions, besides his teachings in other chapters.

Such rituals prescribe how the **Superior Man** or 'gentleman' should behave when dealing with other people (as a means of exercising self-control by directing his emotions in the right direction).

For example (*Analects* 16:10), the **Superior Man**

In regard to his...
♦ eyes

Is anxious to...
♦ see clearly

◆ ears	◆ hear distinctly
◆ doubts	◆ question others

In regard to his...	**Is anxious to be...**
◆ countenance	◆ benign
◆ demeanour	◆ respectful
◆ speech	◆ sincere
◆ business	◆ reverently careful

When he...	**Thinks of...**
◆ is angry	◆ the difficulties his anger may bring him
◆ sees gain	◆ righteousness

and, immediately before the Golden Rule:

> 'The superior man in everything considers **righteousness** to be essential. He performs it according to the rules of **propriety**. He brings it forth in **humility**. He completes it with **sincerity**.'

When combined with benevolence (*rén*), such rites acquire human meaning rather than being merely hollow gestures.

From these rites stem the rules governing Chinese accepted standards of behaviour that foreigners will encounter in **business etiquette**, which are fully described in subsequent chapters.

POLITICAL ENVIRONMENT

China is a multi-party, multi-national state under the leadership of the Communist Party of China (CPC).

To quote the current constitution (of 1982) the PRC is:

> 'A socialist state under the people's democratic dictatorship led by the working class and based on the alliance of workers and peasants.'

This is the '**socialism with Chinese characteristics**' into which Communism has evolved in China, as described below.

Communism

The origins, aims and development of Communism in general are too well known to recite here.

Suffice it to say that, since the communist revolution and founding of the PRC in 1949 under **Mao Tse-Tung**, China is one of only a handful of countries where communism has survived as the ideology of a nation state. This is probably due to China's continually adapting communism to suit her own needs, rather than copying the Soviet ideological model as most other communist countries did.

Maoism

Mao preached a peasant type of Marxist-Leninism, with a principally rural and military outlook that reflected his own background.

Thus, in his desire to adapt communism to suit China's needs, Mao:

◆ promoted **land reform**

◆ ascribed a greater role to **agriculture** and the **peasantry** in the building of socialism.

Unfortunately, the latter led to the ill-fated:

◆ **Great Leap Forward** (1958), which included reorganising agriculture into collectives, ultimately causing widespread famine

◆ **Cultural Revolution** (1966), intended to:
  – purge Chinese communism – with the support of the People's Liberation Army (PLA) – of the bourgeois influences of the upper middle class (such as art and academia), many of whose members were conscripted into agricultural labour
  – re-establish Mao's supremacy, that had been weakened by the failure of the Great Leap Forward.

The predominant manifesto was the **Little Red Book** of Mao's thoughts, with the rubric by his then heir-apparent (Lin Piao) to 'study Chairman Mao's writings, follow his teachings and act according to his instructions' (*Quotations from Chairman Mao Tse-Tung*, Foreign Languages Press, Beijing, 1966).

On a personal note: how many undergraduates in Western Universities at that time, like me, bought a copy merely out of intellectual curiosity without any regard for its practical impact on the Chinese people?

Similarly, in stark contrast to his contemporaries, Mao maintained that, once economic revolution had been achieved, the state should remain the dictatorship of the proletariat rather than become the state of the entire people.

China today

However, such was the ensuing chaos that, after Mao's death (in 1976), the Cultural Revolution was officially criticised, the leaders sanctioned, and the many innocent victims reinstated – including **Deng Xiaoping**, who eventually succeeded Mao and in turn nominated **Jiang Zemin** and **Hu Jintao** to follow him and in that order (1997 and 2002, respectively).

The main proponent of '**socialism with Chinese characteristics**', Deng advocated reform in place of revolution, but only of the economy: democracy was not an option.

For example: one of Deng's early reforms was to introduce the **Responsibility System**, under which collectives were dismantled and farmers allowed to sell spare produce on the open market.

After his death (in 1997), the CPC declared **Deng Xiaoping Theory** its guiding ideology.

The reason why Deng succeeded where his predecessor failed lies in the main differences between the ideologies of:

◆ **Mao**
 – 'Better red than expert.'
 – ideology is more important than ability.

◆ **Deng**
 – 'It doesn't matter if the cat is black or white; what matters is how well it catches mice.'
 – ability is more important than ideology.

Quotations from *China Basics – Brief History of China,* ChinaTour.com, 2002

Economically, China has been transformed from a planned system into a '**market economy with Chinese characteristics**' (which the cynics might say is a euphemism for 'capitalism'), including gradually opening to the outside world.

The pace of political change, however, is another matter: China has learnt from Russia the danger of simultaneously reforming economic and political systems. Nevertheless, the inextricable relationship between a country's economy and the political system within which it operates means that one cannot mark time for very long while the other continues to move forward.

China tomorrow

According to the *China Daily* (16th Party Congress, www.chinadaily. com.cn), in his report to the 16th CPC National Congress (in November 2002), as the retiring leader, **Jiang Zemin** outlined the following objectives for China's development and reform – 'to:

♦ hold high the great banner of **Deng Xiaoping Theory**

♦ fully act on the important thoughts of **Three Represents** – that is, the Party must always represent the:
  – development trend of China's advanced productive forces
  – orientation of China's advanced culture
  – fundamental interests of the overwhelming majority of the Chinese people

♦ carry forward the Party's cause into the future

♦ keep pace with the times

♦ build a well-off society in an all-round way

♦ speed up socialist modernisation

♦ work hard to create a new situation in building **socialism with Chinese characteristics**'

♦ and 'adhere to the **Four Cardinal Principles**:
  – keep to the socialist road
  – uphold the people's democratic dictatorship
  – uphold leadership by the Communist Party
  – uphold Marxism-Leninism and Mao Tse-Tung thought'.

At the same time, as part of the drive to reform government in general and combat **corruption** in particular, Jiang urged adherence to the **Eight Dos and Don'ts**:

1. 'Emancipate the mind and seek truth from facts; do not stick to old ways and make no progress.

2. Combine theory with practice; do not copy mechanically or take to book worship.

3. Keep close ties with the people; do not go in for formalism and bureaucracy.

4. Adhere to the principle of democratic centralism; do not act arbitrarily or stay feeble and lax.

5. Abide by Party discipline; do not pursue liberalism.

6. Be honest and upright; do not abuse power for personal gains.

7. Work hard; do not indulge in hedonism.

8. Appoint people on their merits; do not resort to malpractice in personnel placement.'

So much for future theory; meanwhile, we will just have to wait to see how things work out in practice. Nevertheless, the current climate for continued economic change, government reform and anti-corruption should bode well for foreign business.

Corruption

Reference is made above to **corruption** – or rather its eradication – in politics; and again below in the context of China's economic reforms and future.

According to Timothy Ong, Chairman and Publisher of *Asia-Inc* (Feb 2003):

> If there is any issue...that is guaranteed to enrage Chinese, it's **corruption**... Corruption figures... as the major challenge for the fourth generation of party cadres...Party leaders are acutely aware that runaway corruption can galvanise popular support against their regime.

That the leadership is serious about eradicating corruption is best illustrated by the personal probity of Zhu Rongji, who, when Premier:

- 'once told subordinates to prepare 100 coffins for corrupt officials and one for himself in the event he was shot in the battle against them' (*Ong, ibid)*

- at the 2002 National People Congress, harshly censured the lavish lifestyles of those officials who 'compete with each other to celebrate festivals in the most extraordinary manner' and 'use public funds to dine in fine restaurants and for private travel abroad' *(Ong, ibid)*.

Examples

For example, during February 2003, when I was in Shanghai, the national and local press carried the following reports:

- A 'former vice-president of xxx University. . . has been sentenced to 10 years in jail for bribery. . . From 1996 to 1999 he received. . . a US$200,000 bribe from a contractor' (*Shanghai Star,* 13 Feb 03).

- 'A former police head in xxx was executed. . . for bribery and illegal possession of weapons and ammunition. From November 1995 to early 1999, X pocketed more than RMB 1.8m (US$217,000) from a local gambling ring' (*Shanghai Daily*, 15 Feb 03).

- 'During the past five years (1998–2002), procuratorial departments at various levels in the country have cracked down on more than 200,000 cases of abuse of power involving more than 10,000 officials of above county and division levels. It has retrieved pecuniary losses of US$2.4b for the country' (*China Daily*, 18 Feb 03).

- 'Nearly 68% of the corruption cases investigated by local prosecutors over the past five years (1998–2002) involved SOEs, eliminating a threat to the development of the state sector' (*Shanghai Daily*, 19 Feb 03).

- 'Jade articles seized from officials convicted of corruption. . . were displayed yesterday. . . The convicted officials included X, former mayor of xxx, who has been sentenced to death pending two years' probation; and former vice-mayor Y, who has been executed' (*China Daily*, 20 Feb 03).

Big Brother

One of the less pleasant aspects of a dictatorship is the '**Big Brother**' syndrome as portrayed in George Orwell's *Nineteen-Eighty-Four*, where the portrait of the party leader, who never appears in person, dominates every public place. Of what does that remind you: Mao's portrait overlooking Tiananmen Square, perhaps?

For example, it is said of China that:

- lifts in hotels and public buildings have ears
- security guards in foreign housing compounds are the eyes and ears of the Public Security Bureau (PSB)
- the PSB intercepts all e-mails
- certain subjects are taboo, as discussed in Chapter 3.

Nevertheless, my family felt more at ease in China in the late 1990s than when living in Spain under the Franco regime – as follows:

1. Within only a week of arriving in China, my wife traded her Christian beliefs for the first-hand experiences of a student in the Tiananmen Square incident.
2. I have enjoyed (apparently) unfettered internet and e-mail access from, to and within China for several years.

To those foreigners who 'keep their nose clean', whether Big Brother is or is not watching should be of no concern. Any who behave otherwise, as they have found to their cost, may attract the unwanted attention of the public security agencies, as they well might elsewhere in the world. Thus, to be on the safe side: '*ru xiang, sui su*' ('enter village, follow customs' – the Chinese equivalent of the Latin proverb 'when in Rome, do as the Romans do').

ECONOMIC ENVIRONMENT

For the sake of its currency and relevance, this section is more an overview of the environment in which China's economy operates, than a review of the economy per se.

Iron Rice Bowl

Just as Confucius advocated that the responsibility of government is to provide food, security and education for the people – so Mao's government, in its early years, promised workers an **iron rice bowl** (*tie fan wan*) of lifetime employment, housing, health care, pensions and education provided by employers.

Naturally, some strings were attached, as follows:

♦ jobs were allocated, rather than chosen; and not always consistent with employees' abilities or location.
  For example:
  – a colleague of mine, on graduating in engineering, was sent by the authorities to a pharmaceutical laboratory
  – my wife's Chinese tutor abandoned medicine in order to stay with his wife, also a doctor, when they were posted to different cities
  – on completing their degrees, the students with whom I associated were selected by future employees on the basis of their tutors' recommendations

♦ unmarrieds were expected to live with parents

♦ movement of labour was restricted

♦ serious transgressions could be punished by the withdrawal of employment and hence denial of access to such provisions – for example: parents of illegitimate children or more than one child, and professing Christians.

However, in line with China's economic reforms (described below), this cradle-to-grave provision by the state is being gradually phased out to be replaced by a greater personal self-sufficiency.

Which raises two questions: in the future, who will (1) provide and (2) pay for unemployment, housing, hospitals, pensions and schools? The strain on these will be exacerbated by people moving from the countryside to the cities as residency restrictions are gradually lifted.

The answer to the second question affords **foreign financial services providers** a golden opportunity to satisfy a burgeoning market need (assuming the conditions are right).

Economic reforms

In 1998, under the then Premier **Zhu Rongji**, China embarked on ambitious plans to restructure loss-making **State-Owned Enterprises** (SOEs) in order to:

◆ improve productivity and efficiency; and thereby...
◆ maintain competitiveness in a socialist market economy.

To cure an ailing command economy with modern commercial principles is no ordinary task – but then Zhu was no ordinary Prime Minister, since he was:

◆ the first economist in the PRC's history to hold that office
◆ recognised as the most able manager of the economy
◆ the leading proponent of a market economy
◆ a convenient scapegoat for Jiang, if the reform of the SOEs did not go according to plan.

SOEs affected included the:

◆ state-owned commercial banks and the **People's Bank of China** (PBOC), the restructuring of which would lay the foundation of a modern financial system and regulatory framework, respectively, to suit the needs of a socialist market economy at home and abroad. In particular, the PBOC would be split into two to separate the roles of regulating lenders and setting monetary policy

◆ **government**: by abolishing ministries managing specific industrial sectors – a relic of a planned economy that would be an anachronism in, and hindrance to, China's new socialist market economy – and reforming them into regulatory authorities under an enlarged **State Economic and Trade Commission** (SETC).

At the same time Zhu affirmed that China would:

◆ maintain her **open door policy** to foreign business, including extending access inland from the Special Economic Zones (SEZs) and open coastal cities

◆ improve the **investment environment**

◆ eradicate **corruption**, now re-classified as an '**economic crime**'. (It is no exaggeration to say that one method of dealing with the chief executive officers (CEOs) of poorly performing state industries has been to execute them.)

Economic future

According to the *China Daily*, in his report to the 16th CPC National Congress (in November 2002), as the retiring leader, **Jiang Zemin** outlined the following objectives for China's economic development and reform during the first two decades of the twenty-first century – to:

♦ improve the socialist market economy
♦ promote strategic adjustment of the economic structure
♦ basically accomplish industrialisation
♦ energetically apply IT
♦ accelerate modernisation
♦ maintain a sustained, rapid and sound development of the national economy
♦ steadily uplift the people's living standards.'

To these ends, Jiang proposed the following eight strategies – 'to:

1. Take a new road to industrialisation and implement the strategy of rejuvenating the country through science and education and that of sustainable development.' As regards sustainable development, he stressed 'adherence to the basic state policies of **family planning** and environmental protection.

2. Make the rural economy flourish and speed up urbanisation.

3. Advance the development of the western region and bring about a coordinated development of regional economies.

4. Stick to and improve the basic economic system and deepen the reform of the state property management system.

Future of private and public enterprise
Of special interest to foreign firms looking to invest in China are Jiang's comments on the future of China's private and public enterprise:

'In line with the requirements of releasing and developing the productive forces, China must:

◆ uphold and improve the basic economic system

◆ stimulate the **development of the non-public sectors** while keeping the public sector as the dominant player, incorporating both into the process of the socialist modernisation drive instead of setting them against each other

◆ improve the government functions of **economic regulation** and **market supervision**

◆ deepen the **reform of SOEs** and further explore diverse forms for effectively realising public ownership, especially state ownership.'

5. Improve the modern market system and tighten and improve macroeconomic control.

6. Deepen the reform of the income distribution system and improve the social security system.

Future of China's social security systems
Of special interest to foreign financial services providers are Jiang's comments on the future of China's social security systems:

'Efforts should be made to improve the basic **old-age pension** and **medical insurance** systems for urban workers and the systems of **unemployment insurance** and subsistence allowances for urban residents.'

7. Do a better job in opening up by 'bringing in' and 'going out'.

Future of China's international trade
Of special interest to foreign firms looking to trade with China are Jiang's comments on the future of China's international trade: 'In response to the new situation of economic globalisation and China's entry into the WTO, China should:

◆ take part in **international** economic and technological cooperation and competition on a broader scale, in more spheres and on a higher level

- make the best use of both **international** and domestic markets

- accelerate reform and development by **opening up**

- strive to **increase exports** by ensuring good quality

- attract more **foreign direct investment** and use it more effectively

- encourage and help relatively competitive Chinese enterprises with various forms of ownership to **invest abroad** in order to form a number of strong multinational enterprises.'

8. Do everything possible to create more jobs and improve the people's lives.

Future of China's workforce
Of special interest to foreign firms looking to trade in China are Jiang's comments on the future of China's workforce:

'China should:

- introduce flexible and diverse forms of employment

- encourage people to find jobs on their own or become self-employed.

Entrepreneurs and technical personnel employed by **non-public** scientific and technological enterprises, managerial and technical staff employed by **overseas-funded** enterprises. . .**private entrepreneurs**. . .**free-lance professionals**. . .are all builders of **socialism with Chinese characteristics**.'

These are not hollow words and any sceptics who think otherwise should first consider that China's **Gross Domestic Product** (GDP) in:

- *2002*: grew by 8% (according to the National Bureau of Statistics) – making China the sixth largest and the fastest growing large economy in the world (according to the International Monetary Fund) and second only to Japan in Asia

- *2003*: should grow by 7.5% to 8% (according to the World Bank and State Information Centre, respectively) – with estimates in between from the State Development Planning Commission (SDPC) and Academy of Social Sciences

whilst the Consumer Price Index (CPI) for 2003 should rise by no more than 1% during 2003 (*China Daily*, 18 Feb 03).

Bureaucratic restructuring

Further major reforms of the economy's bureaucracy will follow the change of leadership in March 2003 – including the merger of the **SETC** and **Ministry of Foreign Trade and Economic Co-Operation** (MOFTEC) into a new Ministry of Commerce (*China Daily*, www.chinadaily.com.cn, 06 Mar 03).

Although such reforms should benefit foreign business in the long run, they may cause momentary inconvenience whilst the supervision of Foreign Direct Investment (FDI) beds down in its new home.

Financial systems

A successful economy needs a sound financial system – which China has, despite a high Non Performing Loan (NPL) ratio, according to the former Governor of the PBOC (Dai Xianglong) (in *Beijing Review*, 16 Jan 03, 37) for the reasons that 'the:

- Chinese economy has maintained rapid and sustained growth

- value of the Renminbi (RMB) remains stable

- foreign exchange reserves have kept rising at a fast pace

- various indictors of external debt are far below the universally accepted warning limits

- proportion of the extended public sector borrowing to the GDP is below the international warning line

- securities market and insurance industry are developing in a regulated way

- NPL ratio of financial institutions is declining

- public has high confidence in the development of the country's banking industry and reforms'.

Outlook for foreign business

So much for future theory; meanwhile, we will just have to wait and see how things work out in practice.

Nevertheless, the current climate for continued economic change, government reform and anti-corruption should bode well for foreign businesses that might otherwise have been deterred by the uneven playing-field between them and domestic companies caused by the:

◆ lack of effective, transparent and consistent market regulations

◆ regulators also trading as competitors

◆ burden of government bureaucracy

◆ over-protection of domestic industries

◆ non-competitiveness of the market

◆ fear of corruption.

There will also be a need for **foreign experts** from many walks of life to help manage the change.

Private enterprise

Privately Owned Enterprise (POE) and wealth are booming in China, as evidenced by:

◆ Also in 1998: the founding by the **All China Federation of Industry and Commerce** of China's first private bank, the Minsheng, as a further boost to private enterprise which, by the end of that year, accounted for 26% of China's Gross Domestic Product (GDP) (according to figures published by the Research and Development Centre of the State Council).

◆ At least one Chinese businessman figuring amongst the richest 500 people in the world (according to one poll published in the West).

◆ The admittance, for the first time, of senior POE managers as representatives to the 16th CPC Congress (in November 2002) – thereby giving political recognition to the status and functions of the non-State and private sector and, hopefully, removing major obstacles to its development.

♦ The prediction, following the same Congress, that POEs could account for 50% of China's GDP by the end of 2003.

EXAMPLES

I can confirm that private enterprise and wealth are booming in China – as when in the late 1990s I bought a:

1. Mercedes in Beijing, the only other customer in the car showroom was Chinese
2. basset puppy from the PLA Dog Breeding Unit in Champing, I had difficulty haggling down the price from US$1,600 to US$1,100 in RMB equivalent
3. set of four antique chairs from a private dealer in Beijing. I successfully negotiated down the price from RMB 20,000 to RMB 12,000.

One child policy

As the world's most populated country, China is faced with the problem of feeding about 20% of the world's population living on approximately 5% of the earth's cultivatable land surface.

One solution, since the late 1970s, has been to restrict married couples to having only one child, with severe penalties for additional or illegitimate children.

The negative **social consequences**, well-documented in the West, range from inconvenient to inhumane, such as:

♦ a generation of only sons, nicknamed 'little emperors', who, as conscripts, cannot make beds or tie shoe-laces (according to the *China Daily* and London's *Daily Mail*, respectively)

♦ one in seven of these may never marry, due to too few prospective wives as a result of the alleged abortion of female foetuses and abandonment of baby girls.

The negative **economic consequences** include the same increasingly ageing population that the rest of the world is also facing due to longer life expectancies. Currently (according to the 2000 census), 7% of China's population is aged over 65, and the average life expectancy is 71 years. By 2040, however, the United Nations (UN) expects that proportion to exceed 20% (*Asia-Inc*, Feb 03, 21).

In China, however, this situation is exacerbated by the 'triple-whammy' of the:

1. preceding '**baby-boom**' (encouraged by Mao)

2. withdrawal of the '**iron rice-bowl**'

3. emergence of China's 'Dinky' (double-income no kids yet) or 'Chuppy' (Chinese young urban professional) generation, who are delaying parenthood.

Consequently, the country is threatened by the spectre of a growing number of elderly people with little or no means of support having to rely on a dwindling pool of progeny – the so-called '**pivot generation**'. They in turn need to support themselves and their dependent children in the face of increasing unemployment following the reform of the SOEs.

The situation is particularly critical in **Shanghai**, where the **birth-rate** (according to the Shanghai Population and Family Planning Commission) has:

◆ been consistently below the national average since the introduction of the '**one child policy**'

◆ dropped sharply by one-third between 1990 and 1996

◆ bottomed out to approximately half the national average at the end of 2002.

The reasons given by the Commission include:

◆ career plans, with many women having already earned crucial, highly paid positions with their employers

◆ a higher female employment rate than in other parts of China

◆ the cost of raising children in Shanghai which is more expensive than in other regions of the country

◆ keen social competition that prevents women taking maternity leave, and/or bosses who break or bend the law to pressure them not to do so – despite their having the right to nine months' leave, without losing their job or being transferred to a less important position.

According to a survey by Fudan University in 2002, one in eight married Shanghainese couples under 40 years of age had chosen to have no children (*Shanghai Daily*, 15 Feb 03):

> This trend is a reflection of the changes in the **value system of the Chinese**, especially young people. Children are no longer viewed as a link to maintain the family and a family without children is not considered an unhappy or at least incomplete family. Young people are starting to value their career development and life quality more, instead of the so-called social responsibility.

Until recently, such a viewpoint was an anathema in China, where the sense of the extended family has been so strong (the legacy of Confucian '**filial piety**') that it would have been inconceivable for grown-up children to negate their duty – affection does not enter into the equation – towards helpless parents for younger dependents.

Indeed, as recently as the late 1990s, a survey by an American insurer, again in **Shanghai**, revealed the following:

Priorities of professional men in their mid-30s		
Order	**Whom?**	**What?**
1.	parents	long-term care
2.	children	education
	children and themselves	health care
		housing
3.	themselves	pension

Who is going to build the schools, hospitals and houses, provide school fees and health insurances, mortgages, mortgage protection, and pension plans? Not to mention maternity and child care, funerals, unemployment and holidays? Surely, here is an opportunity for foreign business!

EXAMPLE

In 1998: I was invited to invest in the construction of a new school and hospital, as well as a major civil engineering project.

Meanwhile, as recently as November 2002, the 16th CPC National Congress reiterated adherence to the basic state policy of **family planning**.

Nevertheless, in early 2003, new legislation was introduced allowing **parents who are both only children** to have two offspring. Viewed logically in purely mathematical terms, the population might otherwise suffer significant reversal, if each generation were to reproduce no more than half itself.

Unemployment

Unemployment has already been alluded to above. To put it into context, unemployment among the registered urban workforce reached 4% at the end of 2002 (*China Daily*, 19 Feb 03). This figure is likely to rise – for example (according to the *China Daily*, 17 Feb 03): in Shanghai during 2002:

◆ job applicants grew at an approximately 40% faster rate than job vacancies (about 50% and 35%, respectively)

◆ university enrolments (i.e. future graduate job-seekers) rose by just over 30%.

Thankfully, **unemployment insurance** is catching up slowly, especially in the non-State sector – as illustrated by the fact that (according to the Ministry of Labour and Social Security) at the end of 2002 the number of policyholders was:

◆ c.35% higher than in 1989
◆ split virtually 50:50 between SOEs and POEs.

One instance of the West's contribution to developing such insurance further is the three-year Sino-British Unemployment Insurance Project, launched in February 2003.

OPEN DOOR POLICY

In 2001, China successfully negotiated to:

◆ join the **World Trade Organisation** (WTO)
◆ host the **2008 Olympics**

both of which not only represent positive steps forward in her international relations; but also confirm and advance China's '**open door policy**' (*dui wai kai fang*) to foreign businesses and investors, due to the:

♦ free-trade ethos of the former
♦ infrastructure requirements of the latter.

World Trade Organisation

Provided she abides by its agreements and her promises – which I have no cause to doubt – China's membership of the WTO should make it easier for foreigners to do business with the Chinese, by:

♦ further opening and de-restricting her economic environment (described above)

♦ creating a more predictable environment for foreign investors.

Indeed, at the end the first year of membership (2002), China passed the WTO's annual review, including the fulfillment of her WTO commitments.

Inter alia, China agreed to:

♦ reduce **tariffs** (in 2002: achieving cuts on over 3,000 items and reducing average rates from about 15% to 12%, with a further 1% reduction expected in 2003 – according to the Ministry of Finance); and remove **non-tariff** barriers

♦ extend equal treatment and status to Chinese and non-Chinese companies; and not discriminate between them

♦ desist from **dual-pricing** goods for domestic sale and export; and from using **price controls** to protect domestic industry

♦ end **export subsidies** for agriculture; and lift **subsidies** for agricultural production

♦ open up **services** to foreign competition (e.g. telecoms, banking, insurance)

♦ revise existing and promulgate new laws to comply with her agreements.

Foreign investment

Since being admitted to the WTO, a spokesperson for the China Council for the Promotion of International Trade (CCPIT) prophesied – in July 2002 – that the:

♦ amount of FDI should grow steadily and reach US$50 billion during 2002 – more than the rest of Asia combined – which it did, reputedly making China the number one global destination for FDI and the world's second biggest pot of foreign reserves after Japan

♦ focus of FDI should shift, in particular towards developing the services and new and high-tech sectors; and reforming the SOEs

♦ number of foreign-invested companies should increase

which sentiments Jiang Zemin, as the retiring leader, echoed in his report to the 16th CPC National Congress (in November 2002), detailed above.

It may come as no surprise, therefore, to learn, for example, that:

♦ 'Foreign mergers and acquisitions (M/As)...are becoming' such 'a new force driving forward reform in SOEs' that '2002 was regarded as a year of foreign M/As in China' (*Beijing Review*, 23 Jan 03, 22).

♦ 'China is now Volkswagen's second biggest market, having overtaken the US in 2002, and the company plans to...double annual sales to 1 million in 2007' (*Shanghai Daily*, 18 Feb 03).

Travel and tourism

The open door swings both ways – out as well as in – witness the fact that the Chinese are now the fastest growing group of international travellers, following the government's easing of restrictions on obtaining a passport – previously the main obstacle to their leaving China.

Curiously the increase in out- and in-bound travel during 2002 was approximately similar at c. 25% and 23%, respectively (according to the Ministry of Public Security).

Of the outbound travellers: apart from diplomats, businesspeople and tourists, a growing number of Chinese are choosing to work abroad on short-term assignments as a means of making money, setting up future projects or broadening their perspectives before returning home to enjoy a better quality of life long-term in China.

Apparently, in a country where it is not uncommon for family members to have been split by their job allocations (*Shanghai Daily*, 18 Feb 03):

> It makes no difference that a husband and wife live in different cities within China or in other parts of the world' since 'in the internet age, the visual telephone and other modern telecom facilities enable husbands and wives to communicate, narrowing the distance between them.

In this respect at least, the Chinese are no different from Westerners working in the Far or Middle East!

Foreign exchange
At the time of writing, one fly in the ointment that still plagues overseas business in general, and tourism in particular, is the non-convertibility of the Chinese currency, the RMB.

World Expo 2010
Looking beyond the 2008 Olympics, China will further open wide her doors in 2010 to host the world's leading trade exhibition – the prestigious **World Expo 2010**, in Shanghai.

E-commerce
In stark contrast to the situation in the late 1990s – during my time there – when the **internet** was regarded as a potential threat to her integrity against which a new Great Wall should be built, one consequence of China's accession to the WTO has been the lifting of restrictions on the use of the internet domain '**.cn**' (in December 2002).

Consequently, according to a report issued at the same time by NeuStar (*The Next Frontier of Global E-Business*, 4–5, see Bibliography):

'The data clearly shows that success in China can propel the market share of a vendor. Further, China's recent entry into the WTO may introduce more vendors into the market and increase competition. With such a dramatic commercial metamorphosis taking place right now in China, the country is poised to become one of the most dominant e-commerce players in the Asia/Pacific region – and the world.'

Obstacles to e-commerce in China

However, when it comes to paying for goods on-line, there are currently the following obstacles:

1. Unsophisticated banking systems (despite initial incursions into internet banking by such as the Hong Kong and Shanghai Banking Corporation (HSBC)).

2. Limited use of credit-cards.

3. Preference for paying cash.

Long-term commitment

Despite the foregoing, we should not expect China suddenly to fling wide her gates and welcome all and sundry. Were that to happen, there is the real danger – that China fears – of out-moded domestic ventures being destabilised by the superiority of modern foreign adventurers, especially in the financial services sectors.

EXAMPLE

Just compare the sophisticated distribution channels of Western financial services companies with the trestle-tables that I saw the largest Chinese insurer set up on the pavement outside a department store in Shunyi County (near Beijing) in the late 1990s.

The Chinese way is to hasten slowly: the lengthy WTO negotiations proved that! Foreigners intent on doing business must be patient, and prepared for their own **Long March** – which, as Mao said, begins with the first step.

Foreign businesses that grow tired of waiting, and pull out of China thinking they can always return are sadly mistaken. At worst they may be turned away; at best, sent to the back of the queue. Similarly, 'hit-and-run' entrepreneurs who want to make a fast buck. What the Chinese are looking for, individually and corporately, is **commitment to China**, which they will test by deliberately playing waiting games.

What might constitute such commitment, how to demonstrate it, and what first steps to take will be considered in Chapter 9.

Meanwhile, suffice it to say that: the longer you are prepared to wait, the sooner you are likely to arrive.

LEGAL ENVIRONMENT

For the sake of its currency and relevance, this section is a brief overview of the environment in which China's law operates, not a review of the legislation per se.

Law is made for man

As in Christian theology 'the sabbath was made for man, not man for the sabbath' (Mk 2:27), so in Chinese thinking (for which read: Confucian Anti-Legalism): '**the law is made for man, not man for the law**' ('*ren zhi bu shi fa zhi*').

Whilst this approach should theoretically favour the legislated, rather than the legislators, it does have some practical disadvantages – a major one being that until new legislation is published, it is hard to know its content and import.

EXAMPLE
In the late 1990s I had great difficulty getting a firm verbal, let alone written, answer from the authorities to apparently straightforward questions – such as: 'for such and such a joint venture operation, what is the allowed percentage capital split between the foreign and Chinese partners?'

When you ask, more often than not the likely reply will be a Confucian and face-saving, 'we are still thinking about it' (rather than, 'we do not know').

The argument seems to go something like this:

◆ '**If** we (the legislators), based on our current experience, not only firmly make up our minds but also firmly commit our decisions to paper, **then** in the future we are bound to follow our own rules and cannot change them so easily when they do not suit a new situation that confronts us which, had we known about it at the time, might have led us to make a different decision originally.'

It is possible, therefore, that no two answers to the same question may be the same; which could consequently lead to inconsistent practices.

EXAMPLE

In the 1990s: the conditions under which the authorities granted the first few foreign insurance licences were all different.

As a member of the WTO, China now needs to develop a code of commercial law in line with international trade practice, in order to create a more predictable environment for foreign investors – as intimated above – for which she will require help from foreign experts.

EXAMPLES

1. In 1999, I was invited to address the Administration Bureau of the Beijing Government on the regulation of UK insurance intermediaries.
2. In 2003, I wrote a research paper for Shanghai Finance College on the regulation of the UK general insurance market.

It is an encouraging sign, therefore, that – after several abortive attempts over nearly 50 years – a draft Civil Code was submitted to the 31st Session of the Standing Committee of the 9th National People's Congress in December 2002.

Law and '*guanxi*'

As detailed in Chapter 3, life in China functions on the basis of favours exchanged between individuals and institutions, known as *guanxi*.

However, such exchanges increasingly operate within a framework of law and regularised procedures.

According to Apco China (www.apcoworldwide.com):

'Having good *"guanxi"* is essential, but a common mistake is to rely on *"guanxi"* to cut a "special" deal that would not otherwise get done due to conflicts with law or policy. This simply exposes you to a high degree of political risk due to changes in personnel, policies or attitudes. *"Guanxi"* can never compensate for deficiencies in the legal, regulatory or commercial logic of a transaction or investment'.

Copyright
See Chapter 3: Intellectual Property Rights.

APPLICATION
The following topics are specifically referred to again in subsequent chapters, as follows:

Topic	See chapter
Big brother	2, 3
Corruption	3, 4
Eight Dos and Don'ts	3, 10
Filial piety	2, 3, 10
Golden rule of Confucianism: Reciprocity	3, 4, 6, 7
Iron rice bowl	2, 3, 10
Key concepts of Confucianism	3
Key concepts of Confucianism: Generosity	4, 7
Law and '*guanxi*'	3
Legal environment	5, 9, 10
Long-term commitment	5, 9
Maoism	3
One child policy	3
Open door policy	5
Political environment	3
The superior man	2, 3, 5
Unemployment	2

(2)

Social Environment

This chapter presents an overview of the relevant background to the social environment in which foreigners may expect and be expected to work with the Chinese, whether at home or in China, under three headings:

1. First the relevant aspects of the **geography** and **history** that have moulded China's **cultural heritage**.

2. Then the **domestic environment** in which the Chinese of today have been brought up.

3. Finally the relationship that, consequently, the Chinese enjoy with **foreigners**.

It complements the preceding overview of the corresponding business environment in general, referring to the following influences in particular:

Underpinning influences	See chapter
Big brother	1
Face (*mianzi*)	3
Filial piety	1
Iron rice bowl	1
Modesty and humility (*keqi*)	3
The superior man	1
Unemployment	1

Like the previous chapter this one attempts to give a sufficient underpinning knowledge to allow a better understanding and, consequently, practical implementation of the 'how to do what' more effectively when working with the Chinese.

CULTURAL HERITAGE

One certain way of failing at business with the Chinese is to ignore their cultural heritage, as moulded by China's **geography** and **history**, which helps explain their attitude to foreigners, described below.

Geography of China

Western cartographers have traditionally described the world around the Greenwich 0° meridian (in London), with the Americas to the left or West and Asia to the right or East.

Whilst the original purpose of this practice (i.e. to standardise navigational aids for seafarers) is entirely honourable, unfortunately it still:

◆ gives the impression that the world revolves around Europe – which may have been true during the heyday of the various empires (e.g. Roman, Spanish and British), but is no longer so in the twenty-first century

◆ relegates China to the far-right edge or Far East of the world map.

Thus, in Western eyes, China is geographically 'off centre' thanks to a quirk of early maritime map-makers.

However, in the Chinese mind, China lies almost at the centre of the world – with Europe to the left or West and the Americas to the right or East – as illustrated by the following map (China Tour.com):

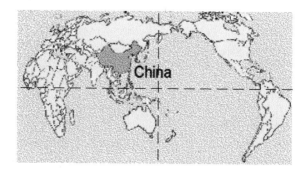

Strange as this may appear to Westerners, it does represent the view that the Chinese have held for millennia that the world revolves around China – as emphasised by its Chinese name *Zhōngguó*'meaning 'The Middle Kingdom', the first character of which is a pictogram of the world with a vertical axis. 中

This world-view (whatever its merits) has been a stumbling block to China's relations with the West in the past, as explained below – and may still be for foreigners who choose to work against, rather than with, it.

History of China

China is one the world's oldest civilisations, with a recorded history of nearly 4,000 years; and boasts the following inventions:

* **paper**

* **printing** with movable type (c.995 AD)

* **gunpowder** (c.1000 AD) – but, in accordance with Confucian pacifism, purely for recreational purposes (i.e. fireworks)

* the **compass** (c.1000 AD), a giant leap forward for navigation.

In **literature**, Confucius' *Analects* (c.500 BC) pre-date by about 1,200 years some of the earliest written literature in English (*Beowulf*), French (*Serment de Strasbourg* and *Cantilène de Sainte Eulalie*) and German (*Hildebrandslied*), all attributed to the eighth or ninth century AD. In other words: on a time-line between Confucius and today, the earliest post-Latin texts of the so-called 'civilized' Western world appear only at the mid-point.

If this surprises today's reader, no wonder that **Marco Polo** was called the Man of a Million Lies when, at the very end of the thirteenth Century AD, he returned to Venice after visiting the court of Kublai Khan, where he discovered **paper money**, **paddle-boats** and a black stone which burns: **coal**.

The Opium Wars

According to the Central Intelligence Agency (CIA) (*World Factbook: China*, www.odci.gov/cia, 2002):

'For centuries, China has stood as a leading civilisation, outpacing the rest of the world in the arts and sciences. But in the first half of the 20th century, China was beset by major famines, civil unrest, military defeats, and foreign occupation.'

However, I beg to differ and, albeit uncomfortably for Western readers, prefer to:

♦ **date** the change in China's fortune to her last 160 years (at the time of writing), or 4% of her recorded history, starting in the nineteenth century AD

♦ **attribute** the cause to not only internal forces; but also the invasion of China by Western traders, as epitomised by the **Opium Wars** (summarised in Appendix 2.1).

Relations with the West

Even the most cursory study of nineteenth century history will reveal the following key insights into China's past relations with the West:

1. **China's attitude to the West** was based on the inability of its ultra-conservative Imperial Qing dynasty to conceive of a community of independent and equal nations. In their view, the world comprised China on the one hand, and the rest of the world on the other – a view that:
   – was so pervasive that Chinese who promoted greater flexibility in China's dealings with the West were accused of being 'Westerners with Chinese faces'
   – still persists today, to a certain point.

2. **The West's attitude to China** in general, and of Britain, France, Germany, Russia and the USA in particular – as the key players – was contradictory, as they simultaneously tried to:
   – **undermine** what they deemed restrictive trading practices, by imposing punitive **Unequal Treaties**, described below
   – **support** the Imperial dynasty, weakened by its defeat in the **Opium Wars**.

Paradoxically, their:
- **objective** was to carve up China for their own purposes
- **strategy** had to be to keep China together.

However, they were thwarted by the outbreaks of the Chinese Revolution (1911) and First World War (1914).

3. By means of such Unequal Treaties, **the West humiliated China** by:
    - **reducing** her to a semi-colonial and semi-feudal country
    - **forcing** her for approximately the next 100 years to replace Confucianism with Western science, technology, industry and management practices
    - **relegating** her to being just one more backward country under the heel of imperial powers (especially Britain, France and the USA).

4. The continual demands by foreign traders for ever-increasing concessions gave rise to **anti-foreign popular uprisings** in China – most notably the Taiping and Boxer Rebellions (1851–1864 and 1898–1900, respectively).

The common link then, as sadly now, is ignorance on both sides.

The Unequal Treaties

All the treaties that the Chinese were forced to sign by the Western powers during and at the conclusion of the Opium Wars – known in China collectively as **The Unequal Treaties** (summarised in Appendix 2.2):

♦ **prohibited** China from isolating herself from the rest of the world

♦ **dictated** her relations for approximately the next hundred years with the West both at home and abroad

♦ **changed** the course of China's social and economic development

♦ **handicapped** the Qing dynasty permanently

♦ **down-graded** the Chinese to second-class citizens in their own country – for example by:

  – banning them and dogs from Huangpu Park in Shanghai's former British Concession

 – subjecting them to local courts presided over jointly by Chinese and foreign judges.

The Chinese looked upon such treaties as unpleasant but necessary concessions dictated by unruly barbarians – who today, sadly, either are unaware of, or choose conveniently to forget, their inglorious colonial past, much to their shame and China's chagrin.

Is it any wonder then that, having been treated so badly, the Chinese may still be cagey about doing business with foreigners; and try to exploit Westerners' remorse for damage their forefathers did to China, as one of their negotiating techniques (described later in Chapter 5).

EXAMPLE

In 1997: I felt very embarrassed and uncomfortable on my first visit with my Chinese driver to the Summer Palace, littered with signs reminding visitors of the atrocities committed by the Anglo-French troops during the Opium Wars.

DOMESTIC ENVIRONMENT

Relevant aspects of the environment in which today's Chinese are brought up are their **attitudes to sex and gender**, **privacy**, **family and friends** and **education**.

Sexual mores

According to Confucius:

'There are three things which the superior man guards against: in youth, when the physical powers are not yet settled, he guards against **lust**...' (*Analects* 16.7a):

which injunction I believe applies to men and women alike, based on the Confucian concept of the soul as sexless.

Not surprisingly, therefore, the Chinese official attitude to sex is still quite puritanical, disapproving of pre- and extra-marital relations. Thus, in the event of a **birth outside wedlock**, the:

- **parents** may be expelled from the CPC and excluded from the 'iron rice bowl'

- **child** may be denied a birth certificate and hence condemned to a lifetime as an illegal – rather than illegitimate – 'non-person'.

EXAMPLE

In 1997: when my adult son and then future daughter-in-law stayed with me in China shortly before their wedding, I was concerned that – for example – the maid might report them to the authorities for 'living in sin', however temporary.

Similarly, and paradoxically, some Chinese may still:

- refrain from and disapprove of public displays of **heterosexual physical contact** beyond a handshake – even between foreigners

- indulge publicly in **same-sex physical contact** – without there necessarily being any homosexual overtones (which is repulsive to most Chinese).

In practice, however, there is increasingly greater sexual freedom than meets the eye, if not a **sexual revolution**. Thus, in 2002 (*Shanghai Talk*, Feb 03, 8–9):

- some 45% of working class males in China report being sexually active before marriage, according to a professor of sexual sociology at Renmin University

- **pre-marital sex** in Beijing reached 70% to 80%, compared with 15% in 1980, according to a researcher at the China Academy of Social Sciences

- **sexually transmitted diseases** were increasing annually at the rate of 30%

and (*Beijing Review*, 23 Jan 03, xv):

- hymen reconstruction is becoming a popular means for brides of restoring their lost virginity

all of which were practically unthinkable only a few years earlier.

Formerly, only some past members of the Chinese leadership reputedly enjoyed dalliances; whilst, as explained later, some interpreters still may be lovers by another name.

EXAMPLES

In the late 1990s, I:
1. was aware of single Chinese of marriageable age (i.e. over 30) clandestinely living together for several years
2. was never made to feel uncomfortable by my Chinese female colleagues when I greeted them with a kiss in private, but never alone; and my wife publicly
3. cannot forget seeing PLA soldiers holding hands!

Foreigners, on the other hand, are perceived to be extremely permissive in this area, as explained below. Suffice it to say that they should not take sexual relationships with Chinese citizens lightly; and even be prepared for rough justice.

EXAMPLE

In the late 1990s: apocryphal stories abounded of foreign men caught 'in flagrante delicto' with Chinese girls, resulting in the latter's punishment.

As a general rule – to avoid being misunderstood and/or compromised: steer clear of situations where you might be alone with a member of the opposite sex (unless your spouse).

Sexually provocative clothing
True to their distaste for public immodesty, the Chinese also object to **provocative clothing**.

Thus **women** should not wear clothes that are excessively revealing – such as plunging neck-lines, see-through blouses, tank tops, hemlines above the knee and shorts.

EXAMPLES

1. My driver was embarrassed by Western females climbing in and out of the car wearing Chinese slit-dresses.
2. My son was annoyed at how Chinese males stared at his wife's skimpy tops.

Modesty applies equally to **men's clothing**.

EXAMPLES

1. Beijing workmen walk the streets in summer wearing only a vest (above the waist) rolled up to their armpits, like a bikini-top, in an attempt to maintain decorum whilst sunbathing.
2. I was stared at when wearing cycling-shorts.

When in doubt: use your common sense.

Sexual equality at work

When it comes to **sexual equality at work**, in my experience China is a model of equal opportunities.

EXAMPLE

I know many well-educated Chinese wives with as successful careers as their husbands, and not always in the same city or even country. A 'trailing spouse' is not a Chinese characteristic. As to the child of the marriage: they may be farmed out to grandparents in a third location.

Nevertheless, although a wife is considered to share the rank of her husband, Chinese spouses seldom show up at social occasions in China.

This has not always been so.

As elsewhere in the world, Chinese women have been subservient to men in a patriarchal and sexist society. But to blame Confucius, as some commentators have, on the basis that there is no evidence that he had any female students is just as specious, in my view, as the arguments for a celibate, male-only Christian priesthood.

Vestiges of the **patriarchal society** do still linger, however, in the way that, for example: Chinese women who drink alcohol and smoke in public are 'not nice'; and drivers still open the car door for the man before his wife.

When it rained, my driver was in a real quandary as to whom he should shelter under the umbrella, despite instructions to give priority to my wife.

Women are also usually the first to be laid off from economically hurting businesses and few business leaders are women.

For example: according to *China Daily* (19 Feb 03):

♦ of the registered urban unemployed for 2002 of 4%, over half were women

♦ amongst female adults under 50 years old, unemployment has risen by c. 16% since 1990.

Who wears the trousers at home?

In the home, however, legislation now protects the wife and favours the virtuous, in that she is entitled to:

♦ after four years of marriage: half her husband's estate

♦ on divorce: additionally, 50% of her husband's half-share – i.e. 75% of his estate in total.

Should the grounds for divorce be his co-habiting with another, however, she is entitled to the whole of his estate and the husband has to leave the marital home – as the Chinese put it – 'only with his trousers'.

Privacy

The Chinese are comfortable with shorter personal distances than many Westerners; and may, therefore, stand a bit too close to you for comfort.

This is because the Chinese – especially those from large and poorly educated families – have little concept if any of privacy or personal space, since it is alien to their home experience.

EXAMPLES

1. My wife experienced Chinese:
   - girl-friends offering to take her to the toilet!
   - maids trying to clean the bathroom while she was using it and joining in her coffee mornings.
2. Recently: Western friends of mine checked into a top-class hotel in China, accompanied by their Chinese host. Shortly after reaching their room, the wife announced she was going to take a bath – to which the Chinese host, by now seated in a comfortable chair, replied: 'Go ahead' without making any attempt to leave!
3. My driver lived in the country in his family's courtyard house that he shared with his: grandfather, parents, unmarried sister, wife and child. Accommodation consisted of a large communal room surrounded by several small bedrooms; outside was a water tap, cooking facility and a screened-off 'hole in the ground' – a far cry from the Beijing show-home *hutongs* that foreign tourists are allowed to visit.

Another explanation for the Chinese apparent disregard for privacy is the alleged **big brother** regime. Paranoid foreigners may, therefore, be excused perhaps for wondering what those service and security personnel who burst into their hotel room unannounced are really after.

Family and friends

The importance of loyalty to family and friends is enshrined in the Confucian concept of **filial piety**.

EXAMPLE

In 1997: one of my Chinese female members of staff resigned only days after joining the company, when her husband's best friend offered her a job. Loyalty to family (her husband) and friends (albeit her husband's) came before duty to employer. As she explained to me: for her to have turned down the offer would have been for her husband a loss of 'face', as explained in Chapter 3.

Erosion of traditional values

Nevertheless, as intimated earlier in the context of the 'one child policy', a new set of social values is being embraced by the so-called 'Chuppies' (*Beijing Review*, 23 Jan 03, xvi):

> 'Now a yuppie class has emerged in China. Young urban professionals, with a handsome income, working like dogs in multinationals and lingering in discos or bars until midnight. They marry late, mostly in early thirties or even older; they prefer DINK (double income and no kids) families; they drink coffee, watch Hollywood movies and listen to Western R&B or hip-hop music, which may be condemned by their parents though. But they don't really care; the older generation is a little out of time (sic). Most of all, fashion is above everything else, because that's the soul of being modern, being a yuppie, at least in appearance.'

By the same token *[ibid]*:

> 'With China's reform and opening up to the outside world, more and more people are celebrating Western festas (sic) while ignoring **traditional Chinese festivals**. Many young Chinese celebrate Western Saint Valentine's Day on February 14, but few of them know the traditional valentine's day of their own country on the seventh day of the seventh lunar month. In fact, many traditional Chinese festivals are meaningful...Each Chinese should have the responsibility to spread Chinese culture to the world.'

And again (*op cit*, 16 Jan 03, xvi):

> 'Chinese tradition is disappearing among Chinese youth. Some are westernised; some prefer Japanese or Korean lifestyles and some even wear clothes with national flags of other countries... Many Chinese children like McDonald's or KFC (Kentucky Fried Chicken) while cannot even use chopsticks well (sic). I have visited many countries and noticed that their children are patriotic and proud of their motherlands. Being Chinese, it is time for us, teachers and parents, to take our responsibilities to educate our children in proper ways, to save our valuable traditions, and to save our country.'

Education system
The Chinese still tend to:

◆ **learn** by rote
◆ **be examined** by multiple-choice tests

methods considered by Western pedagogues to:

◆ **impart** and demonstrate **knowledge**
◆ **stifle** powers of reasoning and **understanding**

respectively.

Such an education system may, therefore, explain why – as foreigners will soon discover during their negotiations and meetings with them, described later in Chapters 5 and 6 – the Chinese:

◆ possess **phenomenal memories**
◆ show **little individual initiative**
◆ prefer **collective decision making**.

RELATIONSHIP WITH FOREIGNERS
As a result of their cultural and domestic environments, the relationship that the Chinese enjoy with foreigners is characterised by their **attitude to** and **perception by foreigners** – which one Chinese commentator (*Beijing Review*, 23 Jan 03, 48) has summarised as: 'Americans are from Mars, Chinese are from Venus' which does not necessarily mean that they are opposites, only different. As the same commentator so aptly puts it: 'We [the Chinese] are ready to be your friends while keeping our characteristics. How about you?'

Attitude to foreigners
On account of their centrism and isolationism, explained above, many **uneducated Chinese** still hold the following outdated attitudes to foreigners:

Foreigners are:

1. Judged by Chinese norms.

2. Not treated as equals, just because they are not Chinese.

3. Considered 'devils' or 'barbarians'.

4. Stereotyped – such as bowler-hatted men stumbling around in the London fog.

5. Stared or shouted at in rural areas – a practice that I, contrary to other commentators, judge deliberately hostile.

EXAMPLES

1. My wife and I, both graduate linguists, were openly ridiculed in rural townships outside Beijing when we attempted to speak Chinese.

2. My then teenage son and I were often shouted at quite abusively whilst cycling in the same rural townships.

3. The Chinese maid employed by my wife gave the impression that she thought the family stupid because we were not fluent in Chinese.

For example: according to various surveys carried out in 2002 amongst China's 'successor generation' (aged 16–35, educated and urban) (*City Weekend*, 13–26 Feb 03, 28):

♦ 'many believed the UK to be:
   – populated by a stiff and reserved people
   – a nation stuck in the past

♦ some saw:
   – the Britons as men in bowler hats walking at a clip with noses in the air
   – doffing servants living below stairs in large country houses
   – regal pomp and circumstance by every turn'.

Nevertheless, as a general rule, most **educated Chinese** are superficially hospitable and pleasant to, but may be wary about befriending, foreigners – since any deeper relationship (such as friendship) would imply mutual obligations, according to the extended Confucian concept of filial piety.

Should a Chinese person befriend you, therefore, beware that their sole aim is not just a ticket or passport to the West.

1. International hotel lobbies are full of middle-aged **foreign businessmen** sporting trophy young Chinese girls on their arms. Rather than be jealous, pity their gullibility: all the girls may want is access to the West.
2. My wife and I strongly recommend married foreign expatriates to take their spouse to China: we have seen too many marriages fail.

The Chinese view of the West is **schizophrenic**, perceiving it as technologically highly advanced, but morally corrupt.

Attitude to foreign women

Thus although Chinese men are not attracted to **Western women**, they do believe them to be promiscuous and thus fair game, so that drivers may 'try it on' while the boss is away. (By the same token, Chinese maids may 'come on' to Western men, while the wife is away.)

In business circles, however, for reasons intimated above, the Chinese show more respect and hold the following attitudes to foreign women:

1. **Foreign businesswomen** are accorded the respect due to their positions.

2. **Wives of foreign businessmen** are welcomed at social occasions (and accorded the same rank as their husbands).

3. **Foreign women** are expected to wear sober clothing, in accordance with Chinese sexual mores, explained above.

4. **Female foreign guests** may drink and smoke in public, even when their Chinese counterparts may not, as intimated above.

This last concession is indicative of the fact that the Chinese expect foreigners to behave strangely!

Perception by foreigners

In the same way as, mentioned above, some Chinese view the West as portrayed by Dickens and Conan-Doyle, so many foreigners' concept of contemporary China is still based on the films of Fu Manchu or *The Inn of the Sixth Happiness*.

For example: according to a Harris poll conducted as recently as September 2002, 56% of Americans considered China 'an unfriendly country'.

I shared this misconception; and was, therefore, pleasantly shocked to find (in 1997) a country in some respects more advanced than elsewhere I had lived in the world – with, inter alia: imposing architecture; attractive shops with high-quality goods; smart clothes; excellent food; luxury cars; and modern technology, with computers and mobile-phones galore!

Above all, I found that people have time for each other. The streets of Beijing were full of people strolling and walking, making the most of every minute – not rushing headlong from A to B to save seconds, as is typical in many Western capitals

That is not to say that all is sweetness and light, despite the best efforts of the foreign-language Chinese press: far from it. Neither is it all doom and gloom, as the Western media would often have us believe. Rather: the truth lies somewhere between, and can only be truly appreciated by an extended stay in China, mingling with the Chinese.

This last point is important. China is not found in foreign housing compounds, bars and club-houses, international hotels, restaurants and shops; sanitised package holidays and city tours; and expatriate-dominated enterprises.

Thus, from my experience in China and elsewhere in the world, beware of the following and avoid expatriates:

1. Whose favourite pastime – especially on a Friday evening in their expats-only club, staffed by Chinese – is **China bashing**, deprecating their Chinese colleagues in no uncertain manner. Bigoted, uninformed, arrogant and wholly out-of-touch with reality – that is why they cannot get on with the Chinese (rather than vice-versa, as they would claim). As explained in later chapters, lording it over the Chinese leads nowhere, except eventually back home. Indeed, one wonders why foreigners choose to interact with the Chinese if all they do is complain about them to other foreigners.

2. Who have **gone native** and spend their Friday evenings running down the home country – do they have a hidden agenda for working abroad?

3. Who say they are going to learn Chinese and about China when they return home: far from being Sinophiles, they display rank ignorance.

Overseas Chinese (huáqiáo)

Although not strictly foreigners, **huáqiáo** (the overseas Chinese) in general, and those from the Province of Taiwan (aka the Republic of China), Special Administrative Regions (Hong Kong and Macau) and Singapore in particular, may nevertheless be treated as such and hence not always regarded as truly Chinese in mainland China.

Neither side is without fault – some:

◆ *huáqiáo*: may not always understand modern Chinese culture, especially as it has developed in China since 1949

◆ *mainland Chinese*: may disapprove of their overseas cousins' affluence, especially if it is flaunted.

Thus it would be erroneous for foreign companies to assume that – for example – by including overseas Chinese in their negotiating teams and/or appointing them as their Chinese CEOs instead of their own country(wo)men, they will enjoy more favourable treatment. In some cases, the result may be quite the opposite.

If this is surprising, just bear in mind the parallel of the UK and USA: two countries divided by a common language!

POSTSCRIPT

Those foreigners who persist in treating China and the Chinese as a 'third world' or developing country that has much to gain from the 'civilised world', should consider the following eight uncomfortable truths about China:

1. If imitation is the sincerest form of flattery: does not the adoption by Western countries of the Chinese imperial model of the civil service, including the word 'mandarin' for a senior or powerful

government official, hold up China as an example to others – in this respect, at least?

2. If China is apparently 'backward' by Western standards: to what extent are those same Western powers who plundered and reversed her ancient civilisation to blame?

3. If China has already 'bounced back' from the aftermath of Maoism to establish herself as the second **world-power** (after the USA), thanks to a whirlwind pace of change akin to the German post-war *Wirtschaftswunder*: how long until she ranks Number One? After all, she is one of only five permanent members of the UN Security Council, having been the very first signatory of the UN Charter. Moreover, at current growth rates, she will catch up the US **economy** by 2020.

4. If you think that the Chinese are 'inscrutable', as many foreigners do, just remember: they may find you equally so!

5. According to *1421: The Year China Discovered the World* (see Bibliography), it was the Chinese who first:
   – discovered what is today the USA (for further details see: Appendix 2.3)
   – occupied the Falkland Islands (aka Las Islas Malvinas) some 560 years before Argentina and the UK disputed their sovereignty.

6. In the same spirit of adventure and discovery, China successfully completed 4 unmanned **space flights** between November 1999 and January 2003; and should launch her first manned flight in late 2003, according to an announcement by the China Aerospace Science and Technology Corporation shortly after the loss of the US space shuttle *Columbia* (in February 2003).

7. Before the announcement of the redevelopment of the World Trade Center in New York (on 27 Feb 03), China had expected to build **the tallest building in the world** by 2007, the 492 metre high Shanghai World Financial Centre. Meanwhile, it is home to the third tallest, the adjacent 420 metre Jinmao Building.

8. In education, the Shanghai-based China-Europe International

Business School MBA programme was ranked amongst the top 50 in the world by *The Economist* in October 2002.

APPLICATION

The following topics are specifically referred to again in subsequent chapters, as follows:

Topic	See chapters
Attitude to foreign women	6, 7
Attitude to foreigners	3, 5, 6, 10
Education system	3, 6, 10
Family and friends	3, 10
Overseas Chinese	10
Privacy	3
Relations with the West	5
Sexual equality at work	6, 7, 10
Sexual mores	3, 6
Sexually provocative clothing	6, 7
The Opium Wars	5
The Unequal Treaties	5

3

Underpinning Behaviours

This chapter introduces the relevant behaviours that underpin the business dealings of the Chinese as a consequence of their business and social environments in general, and the following influences in particular:

Underpinning influences	See chapters
Attitude to foreigners	2
Big brother	1
Corruption	1
Education system	2
Eight Dos and Don'ts	1
Family and friends	2
Filial piety	1
Golden rule of Confucianism: reciprocity	1
Iron rice bowl	1
Key concepts of Confucianism	1
Law and *guanxi*	1
Maoism	1
One child policy	1
Political environment	1
Privacy	2
Sexual mores	2
The superior man	1

Since the remaining chapters not only detail those business dealings but also abound with practical examples of such behaviours, this one includes sufficient examples only to clarify a general point. In addition and by contrast, however, many examples and case studies are given specifically of **working with the Chinese** in anticipation of Chapter 10.

Like the previous chapters this one attempts to give a sufficient underpinning knowledge to allow a better understanding and, consequently, practical implementation of the 'how to do what' more effectively when working with the Chinese.

Ritual behaviour

Although many Chinese are prepared to forgive your lack of expertise – especially the younger and better-educated ones who may have travelled overseas and hence understand what it is like to be on the other side of the fence – there are those who still lay great store on adherence to the rituals of gentlemanly politeness that distinguish the Confucian Superior Man; and for whom outward form may be more important than inward motive.

Hence the reason for devoting so much space in this and subsequent chapters to the correct observance of Chinese business etiquette.

CONNECTIONS (*GUANXI*)

Many cultures and languages have ideas or words that are difficult to express or translate: **guanxi** is one such.

Concept of *guanxi*

In China, *guanxi* is what oils the wheels of life or glues together society in general, and business in particular; and, of the various attempts elsewhere to define it, I commend the following defintions of *guanxi*:

1. '**Relation(ship)**', as between husband and wife, or governments; '**ties, connections**', as in social interactions (*Concise Chinese-English Dictionary*, Oxford University Press, 1986).

2. '**Membership credentials, backdoor connections**' (*New Chinese-English Dictionary*, China, 1996).

3. 'A sort of quid pro quo, "you scratch my back, I'll scratch yours" kind of arrangement' (*Dealing with the Chinese*, Scott D. Seligman, Management Books 2000, UK, 1997, p. 45); 'a tit-for-tat relationship between two people' (*Chinese Business Etiquette*, Scott D. Seligman, Warner Books, USA, 1999, p. 194).

4. 'Something linking two people who in some way have developed a relationship of mutual dependence' (*Encountering the Chinese*, Hu Wenzhong & Cornelius L Grove, Intercultural Press, USA, 1991, p. 61) to which I would add 'and trust' – such as founded in attending the same school or university; or coming from the same geographical origin or lineage.

5. 'A special personal relationship in which long-term mutual benefit is more important than short-term individual gain and contains the key elements of indirect relationship between two people through proper introduction by a third party, and direct relationship between two people who trust each other and the contact person ... It is the mother of all relationships' (*Chinese Cultural Values and Their Implications in Business Transactions*, Wei-ping Wu and Li Yong – in: *Doing Business with China*, Kogan Page, UK, 2000, pp. 192 and 193).

In its simplest terms: *guanxi* is a form of nepotism akin to the **old boy network** or **old school tie** in the UK – but with the added dimensions of:

♦ mutual and obligated dependency, as per the Confucian 'Golden Rule' of **reciprocity**

♦ lasting **for life**.

Hence, it differs from – and, consequently, should not be confused with – the Western practice of networking, which tends to be superficial, short-term, and results-oriented.

Good relationships are so important to the Chinese that they tend not only to treat them as a measure of personal ability and influence; but also to despise anyone who has no connections, and reject them as only half-Chinese.

This applies equally to foreigners, whom the Chinese will expect to understand and follow the rules of *guanxi*; and in reverse – that is: the more a foreigner or 'outsider' builds relationships in China, the more they will be accepted by the Chinese as being one of them or an 'insider'.

My services in China were recognised by my being appointed a Guest Professor at Shanghai's Finance College, then under the aegis of the PBOC.

Rules of *guanxi*

Such rules are:

- the Confucian values of **altruism**, **harmony**, **integrity** and **reciprocity**

- **mutual trust**, **loyalty**, **durability** and **long-term commitment**, intimated above

- **'face'** and **hierarchy**, explained below

for breaking which the penalty is a loss of trust and, consequently, of 'face' leading to ostracism from the network – which in itself is the incentive and self-regulating control mechanism for obeying the rules.

Forms of *guanxi*

There are basically two forms of *guanxi*.

- **Passive form**: acquired through natural means with **'insiders'** – such as via family, school, university, marriage, work, clubs, and neighbourhood etc, as intimated above.

- **Active form**: acquired by exchanging gifts and favours with **'outsiders'**.

For foreigners, it is the second form that they need to observe, according to the practice described below, and the protocol detailed in Chapter 4.

Levels of *guanxi*

There are also two levels of *guanxi*: **personal** and **corporate**.

Whilst *guanxi* naturally originates from the former, for on-going business purposes it needs to develop into the latter, since personal *guanxi* is of value only for as long as the relationship between the individuals concerned remains mutually beneficial and/or inter-dependent. Otherwise, as soon as you or your Chinese counterpart move, retire or die, all that hard work has been in vain, and your successors have to start all over again.

This is not to say that your personal *guanxi* is not important – quite the opposite: it is vital. But you should use it as a springboard to build corporate *guanxi* with your counterpart organisation(s), who will behave similarly. Indeed, some Chinese may not distinguish between the two, and use personal *guanxi* to secure not only personal gain but also corporate advantage.

Thus do not be surprised if an individual Chinese suggests that your and their organisations clinch a totally unrelated deal purely on the basis of your relationship. After all: the prime value to China of building *guanxi* with you – as a 'foreign devil' – is to acquire whatever technology, expertise etc that your organisation can contribute to her progress.

In summary: to be successful, *guanxi* must be as much 'business to business' as 'person to person'.

Foreigners who forget this, and boast of and rely on their personal *guanxi*, do so at their peril.

Practice of *guanxi*

In business, *guanxi* is the **personal networking** that gains you access to elusive contracts, finance, goods, information, markets, people and services by means of exchanging favours rather than money. In other words, it is **not bribery**, given the swift and severe penalties meted out for economic crime, mentioned earlier. Rather, it is a 'circle of friends' who can call on and trust each other to do mutual favours: they for you, and – do not forget – you for them.

Thus, as elsewhere, success in business depends as much if not more on **whom you know**, rather than what – a reality overlooked by those results-oriented foreigners who mistakenly concentrate on finalising contract details rather than spending time building personal and corporate relationships, as the Chinese do, when negotiating business deals.

It is important, therefore, for foreign business(wo)men to understand the following differences:

Problem-solving in China versus the West		
Where	**The problem solver will ask themself:**	
West	**what** can I **do**...	...to solve this?
China	**whom** do I **know** who can help me...	

Hence in China 'business may flow out of friendship whereas, in the West, friendship may flow out of business' (*Doing Business in China*, Tim Ambler and Morgen Witzel, Routledge, London, 2000, p. 198).

However, as I discovered, *guanxi* is not always a function of seniority.

Case Study

In early 1998, I was involved with a tour of China by the Royal National Theatre (NT) of the UK. As a result, not only I but also my wife developed a good relationship with the then Director General (DG) of the Chinese Performing Arts Agency (CPAA) on both a business and personal level – the latter through the various banquets that I organised, where we all were able to indulge our passion for Spanish (see Chapter 7).

Several months later, shortly before I was to take early retirement and leave China, *Turandot* was staged in the open air at the Forbidden City (Beijing). Tickets for half-decent seats quickly became scarce despite being expensive for personal (as opposed to corporate) pockets.

Consequently, I wrote to the DG, in Spanish, fondly recalling our several meetings – mentioning the latter's offer of writing poetry in Chinese for my wife – explaining the situation, and enquiring whether the DG could possibly help obtain tickets.

Unfortunately, no tickets were forthcoming. In hindsight: perhaps I had made an unfeasible request?

Nevertheless, every cloud has a silver lining.

Quite unexpectedly, when (on the evening before the last night) I told this tale to a group of friends, one of them — a Chinese — said, 'I know so-and-so who helped build the stage. He can get you cheap tickets and a pass to the VIP enclosure for tomorrow's final performance'.

And that is how my wife and I came to be sitting in the front-but-one row at a knock-down price, and spending the intervals in the VIP enclosure!

But the story does not end there.

Two years later, I moved house and sent Christmas and New Year (Western and Chinese) cards with our change of address to hundreds of business contacts, including scores of Chinese. I received very few replies (which is par for the course), and only one or two from China — including a message of friendship from the DG of the CPAA!

The most common and straightforward method of using *guanxi* is via 'a friend of a friend'.

For example: if you wish to meet Mr X, and his right-hand Chinese employee has *guanxi* (direct or indirect) with yours, ask the latter for an introduction via that *guanxi*. If successful, your right-hand employee may gain 'face', as explained below, if they were not senior enough to have connected with Mr X without you. This approach is akin to **Newton's Cradle**, using contiguous connections to move up the chain of influence.

Case Study

Whilst writing this book, I was asked by a long-term friend and colleague in London for a contact name in a particular department in a specific Chinese company in China — as follows:

- I contacted...
- my Chinese **ex-Personal Assistant** (PA) in China who offered to ask...
- her Chinese **colleague** to ask...
- her **husband** who had been PA to the Chairman of that company to ask one of...
- his **ex-colleagues** for a contact name in that department...

◆ which was then fed back along the chain to me.

To make the point: although I already knew my ex-PA's colleague's husband, I did not make direct contact for two reasons:

1. I might have offended my ex-PA

2. it is better to use strong rather than tenuous links.

This is a fairly straightforward example – unlike the one quoted by Michael Harris Bond in *Beyond the Chinese Face: Insights from Psychology*, p. 59.

> 'If an individual (X) needs a resource from a stranger (Y), he may be able to obtain it by pulling on his relationship with an associate (Z), who is also associated with Y, so long as Z is indebted to X and Y is indebted to Z. Z may then be able to repay the debt which he owes to X by allowing Y to repay the debt owed to Z indirectly by granting Z's request.'

One word of warning: never forget who it was who acquired a connection for you, or rather 'lent' that connection to you. To take over another's connection without further involving the introducer could cause resentment and close more doors than it opens. Thus, if you continue to meet a friend of a friend, keep the first friend informed and appear eternally grateful: otherwise the latter could turn that friend against you.

EXAMPLE

I was introduced to the Hong Kong General Manager (GM) of a potential Joint Venture (JV) partner by one of my senior Chinese colleagues who had been at University with him. Each time I visited Hong Kong and met the GM I let my colleague know – even when the relationship developed to the point where the GM invited me, my wife and son to lunch.

Which goes to show that: *guanxi* may be hard to build, but even more difficult to recover.

Hazards of *guanxi*

To maintain it, therefore, be sure to keep 'stoking' your *guanxi*, keeping favours in balance. It is not an inexhaustible supply – as some foreigners have mistakenly believed to their cost – but, like a bank account, needs deposits to cover payments.

Otherwise, one of two things may happen – your Chinese connections may:

1. **at best**: withdraw their goodwill

2. **at worst**: pre-empt you by requesting a favour that you cannot grant – for example, ranging from putting in a good word at your Embassy in China to hasten their visa application or at your local university to secure a place (neither of which should cost you money); to paying for their travel or study costs.

Be careful, therefore, not to exaggerate the scope of your *guanxi* in your home country and/or give the impression that such *guanxi* will necessarily yield their desired result. Otherwise you may have to chose between the devil of refusing – with the attendant dangers described below – and the deep blue sea of having to 'cough up'. Fore-warned is fore-armed!

Building *guanxi*

As illustrated above, *guanxi* is hard for foreigners to build, not least on account of the:

♦ **time** needed to establish trust between parties who, as a consequence of their geographical – and possibly linguistic – separation, may meet and/or have direct contact only infrequently

♦ Chinese **attitude** towards them.

Meanwhile, in order to 'prime the *guanxi* pump', I suggest you consider the following methods – which can only temporarily kick-start rather than permanently buy into *guanxi*, since, by its reciprocal nature, *guanxi* cannot be bought:

Hints for building *guanxi* from scratch

1. Use the services of an intermediary who:
   – is respected by your country(wo)men and the Chinese alike
   – has established *guanxi* within the business circles you wish to enter.
2. Select local representatives or senior employees on the basis of their *guanxi* as well as ability.

Collectivism

As a result of not only this importance placed on good relationships (*guanxi*), but also their:

♦ extended Confucian concept of **filial piety**

♦ current political heritage in general, and previous collectivism of **Maoism** in particular

♦ **lack of privacy** or personal space

is it any wonder that the Chinese are primarily social beings – that is: members of a group, to which they owe allegiance, rather than individuals?

Combined with the emphasis, explained below, on:

♦ **harmony** to save '**face**'
♦ keeping a low profile to preserve **modesty**
♦ **obedience** to **hierarchies**

the Chinese put:

♦ group harmony and dynamics before individual behaviour, ambition and assertiveness – which they see as a threat

♦ the preservation of insiders' *guanxi* before the conflicting interests of outsiders – which they do not necessarily consider dishonourable or corrupt behaviour.

For an example of this see Chapter 2 – Family and Friends.

All of this poses the following 'chicken and egg' type question:

♦ Is **collectivism** the result of or impulse for *guanxi*?

◆ Is *guanxi* the result of or impulse for **collectivism**?

Consensus

Add to the above recipe the further ingredient of their uninspiring **education** system and it will come as no surprise that the Chinese prefer **collective decision-making** and **consensus** as a means of taking advantage of **collective wisdom** and building **group confidence**.

Thus, in business, the Chinese will debate issues until agreement is reached on a course of action, and expect individual group members to accept and implement the group decision regardless of their personal views.

Hence, 'agreeing to disagree' is not an option in China.

Intellectual property rights

Confucius disapproved of writers profiting from their work (e.g. by way of royalties or the protection of copyright), contending that the public sharing of knowledge was for the **collective good** of society and, conversely, restricting its use was unhelpful to society. After all, who is to say that person A's idea is original, just because they wrote it down first?

As a result, intellectual property rights (IPR) and similar (e.g. patents) have been regarded in China as unnatural and anti-social – until recently, that is.

With the emergence of digital technology and mass-copying techniques, the Chinese have had to introduce appropriate regulation, which is good news for foreign businesses who might otherwise be deterred by being exposed to what they would consider – but the Chinese used not to – as plagiarism.

FACE (*MIANZI*)

The concept of 'face' differs between distinct languages and cultures.

In China, 'face' (*mianzi*) has been variously:

◆ translated as: '**self-respect**', '**prestige**' and '**reputation**' (*Concise Chinese-English Dictionary* and *New Chinese-English Dictionary*) and '**honour, integrity, privilege, respect and courtesy from others**'

(*What is it in the face?* welcome-to-china.com, 2002)

◆ defined as: '**the regard in which one is held by others or the light in which one appears**' (*Dealing with the Chinese*, Scott D. Seligman, Management Books 2000, UK, 1997, p. 50); '**an intangible commodity that is vital to a person's reputation, dignity and prestige**' (*Chinese Business Etiquette*, Scott D. Seligman, Warner Books, USA, 1999, p. 198).

In other words 'face' to a Chinese person is quite simply their '**status**'; and to lose it, and incur shame, is the worst thing that can befall them.

Whilst this may seem similar to elsewhere in the world, what distinguishes 'face' in China from other cultures is that it can be:

◆ not only lost, saved or won
◆ but also given by others, as explained below.

Losing and saving 'face'

It follows that you should never treat the Chinese – friends, colleagues or strangers – in any way that would publicly demean them, as summarised below, and thus would cause them to '**lose face**'.

Otherwise, you run the very real risk of losing their cooperation; suffering retaliation; and losing the respect of bystanders and all those people that the other person tells – which will consequently cause you too to '**lose face**'.

In such an event, seek the counsel of a Chinese intermediary as to how to 'restore face' – both of the other person and yourself.

To '**save face**', therefore, any criticism should be positive, and delivered privately, discreetly and tactfully – that is, in a mutually face-saving manner, à la Western 'one minute reprimand' – which makes a veritable minefield of reviewing and disciplining Chinese colleagues, discussed later in Chapter 10.

Case Study

When I was posted to China in 1997, one of my first tasks was to move the Head Office from Hong Kong to Beijing and amalgamate it with the Beijing

Representative Office.

Immediately, this threatened the 'face' of my female Chinese Chief Representative for Beijing who, until that moment, had been the most senior employee 'running the show' in the capital – having been selected on the basis of *guanxi* as well as ability, as suggested above

To complicate matters, the Chinese law recognised the legal status of Chief Representative for China (held by me) only if a company had five or more Representative Offices in mainland China, which my employer did not.

Consequently, this further endangered the 'face' of my Beijing colleague, if the Chinese authorities insisted on my being redesignated Chief Representative for Beijing and, subsequently, my colleague being relegated to a lower legal status (such as: 'Representative for Beijing').

To resolve the matter, I:

1. Spent several days working alongside and under the tutelage of my Beijing colleague, in order to:
   - establish my own 'face' through personal effort rather than by edict from my employer
   - give 'face' to my colleague by being willing to learn from her.
2. Talked at length and in private with my colleague, giving her 'face', by:
   - acknowledging her achievements
   - confirming her existing rank and accountabilities
   - agreeing future divisions of shared responsibilities, based on our respective strengths
   - sharing my concerns for her 'face'
   - seeking her advice on how to resolve the issue.

As a result, my colleague not only recognised that my role was sufficiently distinct so as not to undermine her own, but also undertook to present a case to the competent authority to reconsider confirming my legal status (which, in true Chinese style, was never confirmed nor not confirmed!)

For the time being, at least, 'face' was maintained.

However, a few months later, when I and my colleague and the rest of the mixed staff (from mainland China, Hong Kong and the UK) moved into brand new premises, the thorny problem arose of allocating private offices in general, and the one next door to mine in particular – which, in line with Chinese 'hierarchism', detailed below, the Chief Representative for Beijing assumed would be hers (when, in fact, I had different ideas for operational reasons).

To resolve the matter, I:

1. Initially allocated to her the office next to mine.

2. Designated the office where I eventually wished to locate her as reserved for my Chinese No. 2, the Deputy Director for China – based permanently in Guangzhou – during anticipated weekly visits to Beijing.

3. Later, when the latter's visits became less frequent, had little difficulty in persuading the Chief Representative for Beijing, as the most senior member of staff locally, to occupy the Deputy Director's vacant office – despite it being the furthest away from my own!

4. Re-assigned the next-door office to a UK expatriate, in order to avoid appearing to show favouritism amongst the Chinese staff.

Once again, 'face' was saved by and for all concerned.

Gaining 'face'
Whilst losing or saving 'face' implies the active involvement of a third party – as described above – gaining 'face' is something you can independently instigate – typically by acquiring status symbols.

EXAMPLE
At Chinese New Year 1998: when I was fortuitously the first person in Beijing to have the new E-Class Mercedes (in brilliant white), it was remarkable how quickly the traffic police made way for me to pass through the milling crowds!

Giving 'face'
In China, as mentioned above, 'face' may be given to someone by a third party – for example, when person A praises person B's work to the latter's boss. In particular, the Chinese lay special store by 'face'

given them by foreigners, whom they may consequently and subsequently regard with particular favour.

Whose 'face' is it anyway?

In theory, based on the Confucian 'golden rule' of **reciprocity**, the Chinese try to protect the 'face' of others as well as their own.

In practice, however: 'face' is so important to them that some may care more about their own than that of foreigners, and try to save the former at the expense of the latter, even their boss. In such an event, the best (i.e. mutually face-saving) defence is to invoke 'face by proxy', explained below.

'Face' by proxy

In the same way – described above – as your *guanxi* with one person also represents the *guanxi* between your and their organisations, your 'face' is also your employer's 'face', and vice-versa.

In certain circumstances, the 'face' that someone wins or loses may reflect vicariously on their known or close associates and/or employer by their 'basking in reflected glory' or 'cowering in reflected shame' – for example: the members of a winning or losing work team.

EXAMPLE

Shortly after I took delivery of a new Mercedes – mentioned above – I was invited to my driver's village house outside Beijing, where I was royally entertained whilst he stood guard over the car in full view of his neighbours.

This is where 'face' meets *guanxi* and **collectivism**, described above: since the actions of individuals reflect not only on themselves, but also on all of their immediate group and close associates, being linked to others' failure could undermine one's own sway, as no one wants to be tainted by failure, albeit vicarious.

On the other hand sharing in others' success may not necessarily build influence.

Saying 'no'

A sure-fire way of upsetting the applecart in your dealings with the Chinese is for you to say, or put them in a situation where they are compelled to say a bald 'no'. (An example of the latter might be asking for an impossible favour.)

Not only will this cause a 'loss of face' for them, with the attendant risks mentioned above, but also shut the door to further discussion for you – since 'no' means 'no' to the Chinese, for whom any later change of mind or heart would be a sign of weakness and, thus, further 'loss of face'.

'No' is the antithesis of *guanxi*, explained above: once broken, a relationship is hard to re-establish.

You should, therefore, try to leave yourself a way out and forward, by taking a leaf out their book and imitating the Chinese as follows:

Chinese tactics for saying 'no'		
	Rather than...	**the Chinese prefer to ...**
1.	bluntly say 'no'	employ **polite excuses** of the 'I will get back to you on that' genre (such as 'so-and-so is inconvenient, being discussed or under consideration')
2.	blatantly disagree	proffer **counter-suggestions** of the 'alternatively, have you thought of so-and-so' type
3.	say anything	**suck in air** through clenched teeth, to give you time to think again
4.	when all else fails	tell an **abject** or **white lie**

Besides, Chinese prefer circumlocution to blunt speaking – a 'fault' they perceive in, and for which they criticise, Western entrepreneurs and negotiators.

Harmony

Although the last tactic may appear underhand by Western standards, it could equally be a case of a dishonourable means justifying an honourable end – such as, sparing the other person's 'face'.

Indeed, unlike in the West, the Chinese do not consider **lying** to be wholly dishonourable if used to avoid conflict and preserve harmony in personal relations, which transcend each party's particular version of the truth, whatever that may be.

EXAMPLE

In my experience some Chinese would rather lie than lose their own 'face', even when the means and the end are equally 'dishonourable' by their own standards – witness the recent SARS scandal in Beijing.

As a general rule: in such cases, the greater good of the other outweighs the interests of self.

Case Study

In 1997: I was supposed to attend a series of meetings between my international CEO and some very senior Chinese government officials, for which arrangements had already been made.

At the same time, a number of European governments – including mine – publicly criticised China's record on human rights.

Consequently, there was a risk that, by way of 'reprisal' and/or out of embarrassment, the Chinese might decide to cancel the meetings and/or field less senior officials.

As luck (?) would have it, the CEO had just broken his leg, which gave him the excuse to postpone the meetings on ostensibly medical grounds, pleading his doctor's instruction not to fly!

To dispel any doubt, he hosted a prearranged dinner for the then Chinese ambassador a few days later with his leg in plaster!

In this way, 'face' was saved all round.

Making mistakes

Similarly, the Chinese will use identical tactics as a 'cover up' – such as when they make a mistake, or do not know, or want to own up to something. For an example, see the film: *The Yangtze Incident*.

Case Study

In late 2002, I briefed a very senior UK government official (of ambassadorial rank) prior to leading a delegation to China to renegotiate a Memorandum of Understanding (MOU) with the Chinese government.

During one of the meetings, the leader of the UK delegation (who subsequently recounted the events to me, whilst I was writing this book) invited his Chinese counterpart to visit a government establishment in Britain, and asked whether he had been there before – to which the latter replied 'yes' when, in fact, he had not.

Shortly after the meeting, the second-ranking Chinese took aside the leader of the UK delegation, and puzzled him for some five minutes explaining how and why the Chinese do not always say what they mean – before eventually reaching the inevitable conclusion that:

When his boss had said 'yes' what he actually meant was 'no'. In other words, his 'yes' was in response to the invitation (i.e. 'yes, I would like to come') rather than to the question (as in: 'yes, I have been already').

In this way was 'face' maintained. The Chinese host had not made a mistake or misunderstood the exchange. His answer was still the same: it just needed to be clarified, to ensure the meaning was unambiguous!

Conflict management

As explained above, 'losing your cool' is not acceptable in China: indeed, it may exacerbate the situation – for example, by making whomever is opposing you even more determined not to grant your request, as well as losing respect for you.

Rather, on the:

♦ one hand: state your annoyance and reasons objectively

♦ other hand: allow the other person a face-saving way out.

One such method is to use a mutually acceptable third-party or **intermediary** to convey bad news – which, in China, is not a 'cop out' under such circumstances, but an acceptable form of **mediation** that saves both parties' 'faces'.

This is especially true when a foreigner needs to give bad news to a Chinese, to avoid the added indignity of 'losing face' to a 'foreign devil'.

Case Study

Unfortunately, I had to dismiss a very senior male Chinese colleague whose sphere of *guanxi* was such that:

♦ antagonising him might result in his bad-mouthing me
♦ not dismissing him could throw doubt on my credibility and integrity

in the local government and business circles.

To ensure a satisfactory outcome for all parties, I:

♦ gained the support of my Chinese No 2, whom I and the colleague trusted and respected
♦ asked him to act as go-between, suggesting that the colleague might like to retire early
♦ subsequently agreed to meet the colleague to agree terms
♦ informed other staff that their colleague had taken 'early retirement'.

Protecting others' face

In summary, I recommend the following guidelines for protecting others' 'face':

Do . . .
♦ avoid **conflict** and preserve **harmony**
♦ resolve **conflicts** privately, discreetly, tactfully and by using positive criticism
♦ ask **sensitive questions** in private
♦ **respect** rank and title
♦ 'give face'
♦ offer a 'face-saving' way out.

Do not...

♦ reprimand, criticise, embarrass, insult, make insulting remarks about, offend, lose your temper with, shout at, behave disrespectfully towards, prove wrong anyone in **public**

♦ say '**no**'.

According to *welcome-to-china.com* (op cit): 'If you are a *Star Trek* fan' which I am not 'think about Worf and the Klingons.'

MODESTY AND HUMILITY ('*KEQI*')

'*Keqi*' not only means considerate, polite and well-mannered, but also represents **humbleness** and **modesty**. It is impolite to be arrogant and brag about oneself or one's inner circle. The expression is most often used in the negative, as in '*buyao keqi*' meaning 'you shouldn't be so kind and polite to me' or 'you're welcome' (*TravelChinaGuide.com*, July 2002: Travel Essentials – Getting Acquainted – Etiquette).

As one of the virtues expected of the Confucian Superior Man, humility has evolved into a series of public displays of modesty, as follows:

Examples of *keqi*	
When...	**the Chinese may say ...**
They serve you a sumptuous and magnificent home-cooked banquet	'I hope you like our simple food: we are very poor and unadventurous cooks.'
You compliment them on their handiwork – for example: painting or model-making	'You flatter me! I took so little care and made so many mistakes that I was going to throw it away because it's so bad.'
You compliment their family's achievement – for example: acting, or promotion	'You're too kind: I don't think anybody else turned up for the audition or applied for the job.'

As Mao said: 'We should be modest and prudent, guard against arrogance and rashness, and serve the Chinese people with heart and soul' (23 April 1945).

Foreigners should follow suit – thus, for example, when complimented on your spoken Chinese, you should reply along the lines of: 'Thank you, but my grammar and pronunciation are very bad' – rather than boast about having a degree in the language from an ivy-league university.

One purpose is ritually to cede superiority to others by praising them and deprecating oneself, in accordance with the practice of hierarchism, explained below.

However, although **ritualistic**, such displays are not necessarily always false modesty or hollow flattery as some sceptics might think. The mere fact that the Chinese bother to observe their code of gentlemanly behaviour when dealing with unequal 'foreign devils' is in itself a sufficient demonstration of genuine respect.

That is not to say, however, that the Chinese do not use **false modesty** or **hollow flattery** - which they may do to put you in your place – such as when you, in halting Chinese, compliment their genuinely excellent command of your language; and they reply: 'But not as good as your spoken Chinese' or 'your Chinese calligraphy makes mine look like a child's scrawl'. Do not be fooled, but check your ego: they really mean the opposite and are just 'trying it on' in line with the Western saying that 'flattery will get you anywhere'.

HIERARCHISM

In line with the extended Confucian concept of **filial piety**, the Chinese are conditioned not to 'kick against the pricks' of social order – and in particular are taught to respect age and seniority, and defer to authority, age and rank.

Dead men's shoes

One way in which respect for age and seniority has traditionally manifested itself is the 'dead men's shoes' method of promotion – that is, you rise through the ranks to fill the gaps left by your elders. In other words: experience and advancement are a function of age not ability.

In the future, this practice may change, according to the eighth of Jiang's 'Eight Dos and Don'ts'.

Meanwhile, the implications for business are:

◆ Rank should correlate to age – for example, bosses are expected to be older than their staff; the leader of a delegation than its members; and senior colleagues than junior ones.

EXAMPLE

In 1997: when I appointed a new Chinese Office Manager, the Chinese accounts clerk resigned because the former was a couple of months younger. For the record: both were single female graduates aged 29.

◆ Remuneration should also correlate to age – for example: older colleagues expect to earn more than younger ones, even if the former are performing identically or worse in the same or a less important job.

◆ Foreign 'high flyers' (such as directors or general managers) who are too young for their seniority by Chinese standards (say, under 50) and thus insufficiently experienced in Chinese eyes, may:
  – at best: not be taken seriously by the Chinese
  – at worst: be misconstrued as an insult by the home office for not appointing someone of sufficient gravitas – an indication of the importance, or apparent lack of it, that the home office attributes to China.

Thus, rewarding and promoting Chinese colleagues on the basis of performance and ability, respectively, can be a minefield, as discussed later in Chapter 10.

One exception to this rule seems to be that young well-educated Chinese working in China for a non-Chinese employer appear to accept young well-paid foreign graduate trainees – probably because the latter are transient, not blocking the former's promotion.

'Laobanism'

'*Laobanism*', a term coined by me – as far as I am aware – to describe the blind obedience to the boss or **laoban**, or the subjugation of truth to hierarchy, is rife; and manifests itself in business primarily as follows:

Rules of '*Laobanism*'	
'*Laoban*' (the boss)	is always right (even if only by virtue of being older and when obviously wrong): that is why they are the boss – otherwise they would not be
	because infallible, never changes their mind, nor should be openly challenged – which would be a loss of 'face', as explained above
	makes and is expected to make every decision – the Chinese workers' means of 'upward delegation'
	probably arrives last and leaves first – and certainly no one should leave until they have done so

Case Study

During my first few months in China, I was very impressed by the Chinese employees' dedication to a company few had heard of when applying for jobs, and whose international head office was half-way round the globe in a country they might never visit.

For example: their attendance was exemplary, never arriving late nor leaving early. Quite the opposite. Indeed, when helping me to draft major strategy papers for, and preparing to receive delegations from, the international head office, they arrived early, stayed as long as needed, and even worked the odd weekend – all voluntarily.

Thus, in my second quarterly management report, I gave them 'face' by praising their efforts in writing to the international General Manager.

Shortly afterwards, following a discussion with my Chinese bilingual PA, it dawned on me that perhaps the staff felt obliged to arrive before and leave after I did.

Consequently, I called the staff together informally, and explained that the reason why I stayed late on certain days was because my wife's then contract with the British Council was outside normal office hours; and my driver and I were waiting to drive her home. But, please, it was perfectly all right for them to go home on time!

For the next few days, the staff did as they were bid; but gradually slipped back into their old ways, despite my emerging from my office at closing-time to encourage them to leave!

Eventually I had resigned myself to the situation – after all, I was getting really good value for money! – but tried to compromise by leaving earlier when I could, and 'celebrating success' (e.g. with a staff meal or outing) when appropriate.

When the boss is foreign and does not understand the Chinese ways, the result may be disastrous – for example: as intimated above, the Chinese staff may stand by and watch the boss make all the mistakes in the book and 'lose face', whilst ensuring they do not lose their own.

It is not unusual for a boss (Chinese or foreign) to be addressed as *laoban* – even long after the relationship has ended – as a means of giving 'face'.

EXAMPLE

My Chinese ex-PA still occasionally writes to me as her 'boss'.

Changing your mind

If, for the average person, changing your mind is a loss of 'face', then, for *laoban* it can be mistaken for a lack of ability or show of weakness – when, in fact, the opposite may be true.

Case Study

As mentioned above, when I was posted to China in 1997, one of my first tasks was to move the Head Office from Hong Kong to Beijing and amalgamate it with the Beijing Representative Office.

This move offered the opportunity to review, inter alia, such Human Resource Management (HRM) issues as: pan-China staffing requirements, allocation of accountabilities and reporting lines.

Accordingly, I consulted senior colleagues (Chinese and expatriate) individually before convening a collective brain-storming session to finalise and agree details.

For the older Chinese staff – with an average age then of mid-40s – this was probably a new and unheard-of method of working, albeit most welcome, despite their predilection for consensus, explained above.

During the coffee-break halfway through the brain-storm, my Chinese No 2, the Deputy Director for China, provided me with some information of which I was previously not aware.

Consequently, on reassembling after the coffee break, I announced that, on the basis of this new information, I wished the team to back-track and reconsider some of their decisions, which they did, in order to reach better ones.

Afterwards, one Chinese colleague (ex-Red Guard) privately expressed total shock at my change of mind.

This was the beginning of my coaching the Chinese management team to develop a culture where they could make and correct mistakes, and change their minds, without losing 'face' in the eyes of their subordinates.

Business hierarchy

In business, hierarchical distinctions (i.e. rank and status) are important to the Chinese and at the root of China's bureaucratic structures.

Ideally, to save your 'face' and that of others, as explained above, you should interact with people of similar rank and, therefore, age. Otherwise, you may detract from the 'face' of a more senior or much older person; or 'lose face' when dealing with a more junior or much younger one.

In reality, however, this is wholly impractical, especially in the quest for *guanxi*, mentioned above – when I recommend that you observe the following rules:

Rules of business hierarchy	
When dealing with people of...	**you should behave ...**
higher rank	respectfully – that is: deferentially and diffidently, even flattering the other and deprecating yourself (as intimated above)
lower rank	neither as if you consider yourself more important than the other person, nor too informally

Within the workplace, junior staff will often ask senior staff to sound out the boss on their behalf, rather than making a direct approach.

EXAMPLES

1. Drivers spend more time with their bosses than many of the staff do — as a result of which it is common practice for employees to ask the driver to bend the boss's ear in the car or to eavesdrop on in-car conversations (so, beware!).
2. One of my senior Chinese colleagues asked a Western colleague, who knew that I was a Christian – a sensitive subject in China, as mentioned elsewhere – to tell me that he shared the same faith (which, in a Chinese organisation, might have cost him his job).

Exercising authority

As a corollary of being conditioned to respect their 'elders and betters', those Chinese who fall into this category expect natural respect in the exercise of their authority.

Consequently, they may feel threatened by those Western modern management practices – such as empowerment and self-directed teamworking – that turn traditional business hierarchies upside down to cast the boss in the role of facilitator with responsibilities rather than leader with privileges.

EXAMPLE

My most senior female Chinese colleague assumed that my door was always open to her, even when it was shut to everybody else; and took great exception to being told by my younger female Chinese PA – to whom, by the nature of the role, my door was always open – that I was incommunicado.

Similarly, some Chinese staff may:

♦ at best: be confused by
♦ at worst: lose respect for

foreign bosses who try to be 'one of the boys'.

Deferring to authority
Self-deprecation and deferring to authority must be interpreted in the foregoing contexts.

EXAMPLE

It was not uncommon for my middle-aged Chinese colleagues to present me with a problem, and expect me to solve it for them. However, they were not normally averse to suggesting a solution, once asked.

On occasions, therefore, the Chinese may fail to recognise and hence take genuine opportunities that you offer to them to behave otherwise in their best interests.

Case Study

Shortly after arriving in China (1997), I reviewed my predecessor's market entry strategy in consultation with senior Chinese colleagues – for whom, as explained above, it was a new but welcome experience.

As a result, I was able to travel to the UK to present to my international head office a revised strategic plan with the full backing of the China market entry team, which undoubtedly contributed to its acceptance.

A few weeks later, I invited my Chinese colleagues to a follow-up meeting with the international GM, during a visit to Beijing.

One by one, to give credit where credit was due (i.e. 'face'), I asked each colleague to present their contribution so that the GM might commend them.

When it came to the turn of a senior male colleague in his late-40s, he immediately deferred to his line manager – the eldest and most senior Chinese colleague (my No 2) – asking him to speak on his behalf.

If this surprised and disappointed the GM and myself, imagine how much more surprised but pleased we were later on when another male colleague of equal rank in his mid-30s challenged the same line manager by taking issue with something he had said as being inaccurate.

The former missed the opportunity to impress the GM: the latter did so without even realising!

Paternalism

Such exercise of or deference to authority is not always limited to work-related issues. The paternalistic nature of the relationship between employees and *laoban* – consequent upon the Confucian concept of **filial piety** – means that the latter may freely advise, or be consulted by, the former about their personal matters.

Such practice contradicts those Western management traditions that advocate keeping personal problems out of the workplace. However, in China, a good boss is one who looks after his employees' general welfare – not out of altruism, but for the **collective good** of the whole staff: a happy worker is a productive one. (For an example, see Chapter 4: Staff Gratuities.)

Conformity and disagreement

From the foregoing, it will come as no surprise to learn that the basic rule *(Michael Harris Bond,* op cit, p. 83) is: 'Honour the hierarchy first, your vision of the truth second.'

Since the Tiananmen incident (of 1989), however, there is less reserve amongst younger Chinese to challenge authority – such as described in the foregoing case study.

Social hierarchy

When discussing jobs and careers – 'safe' subjects, as mentioned below – do not be surprised by an apparently 'inverted' social hierarchy (in Western terms) left over from Maoism.

EXAMPLE
Whilst practising conversational Chinese with my first driver, I struggled to explain that my father had been a doctor, only to be trounced by the driver who replied in English, with obvious pride and superiority, that his father was a peasant!

TABOO SUBJECTS

What constitutes a taboo may depend on the relationship that you and your Chinese counterparts enjoy. If in doubt, as at all other times when dealing with the Chinese, take your lead from them.

Meanwhile, I suggest the following guidelines.

Chinese politics

Do not criticise **Chinese government leaders** or **policies** (past or present), which may offend some Chinese – even if they criticise them to you.

EXAMPLES
I was told in China of:
1. An ex-leader's alleged penchant for large female tractor drivers – by a close colleague.
2. The spoilt only-sons or 'little emperors' resulting from the one-child policy – by a newly-met senior government official (needless to say: father to a daughter!).

Indeed, it is probably better not to discuss **Chinese politics** at all, since your interlocutors may:

- fear getting into trouble if overheard and reported to a local CPC official
- have been asked by that official to vet your political soundness.

EXAMPLE

When I once visited an academic institution, the host delegation was led by their CPC secretary rather than the Dean.

Not until you have been in China long enough to know for certain what you can say to those whom you can really trust should you deviate from this advice.

EXAMPLE

I was very surprised, therefore, when, only a few days after arriving in China in 1997, my then Chinese PA spoke very openly about the Tiananmen Square incident, where she had been present and her then fiancé, a doctor, attended to the casualties.

Meanwhile, besides those mentioned above, you should also avoid those areas of Chinese politics that the West openly challenges, such as: human rights, Tibet, Taiwan, and the treatment of so-called 'dissenters' (e.g. Falun Gong).

Otherwise, you may well find that not only you but also your associates – through 'face by proxy' (mentioned above) – are 'persona non grata' in Chinese business circles.

EXAMPLES

The British and American business communities in Beijing noted a temporary frostiness in the relations with their Chinese counterparts when in:

1. 1997: someone in the UK's House of Commons spoke against China's record on human rights.

2. 1998: the then US President stood on the steps of Beijing's Great Hall of the People and spoke against the Chinese government's handling of the Tiananmen Square incident.

Sensitive subjects

I recommend the following guidelines for dealing with sensitive subjects:

◆ **Foreign politics**, that is: of other countries.
The Chinese tend to refrain from commenting on the politics of other countries – especially those in conflict – probably as a defence mechanism to deter foreigners from discussing Chinese politics.

EXAMPLE

An insider told me that, when confronted by pro-Tibet demonstrators during a visit to London in 1999, the then Chinese President's view was that they were entitled to their opinion.

Should you engage in a discussion on foreign politics, do not make jokes which the Chinese may find equally disrespectful as of about their own.

◆ **Freedom** whether of expression (including the media) or choice of job or abode.

EXAMPLE

When asked in public by a very senior Chinese government official what was the greatest benefit of my job, I replied: 'Being able to resign' -- which is in sharp contrast to the Chinese job allocation system.

◆ **One child policy**
  – Do not ask a Chinese person 'Have you got children?' – since, in my experience, even the most Westernised Chinese may find this question funny, and laugh in your face at your ignorance of the one-child policy.
  – Rather, ask if they have got 'a child?' or even 'a son?' – when you

should be prepared for the Chinese to boast about a son, and lament over a daughter.
- Above all: do not question the causes behind the disparity in the ratio of boys to girls.

◆ **Sex, drugs and crime**
Chinese justice is swift and severe – for example: reputedly, more people are executed in China (including for drug-related crime) than the rest of the world put together, a fact of which they may not be proud and certainly will not wish to be reminded.

◆ **Spiritual matters** such as religion and the supernatural.
- Do not preach your beliefs or invite the Chinese to your place of worship, both of which are illegal in China.
- Nevertheless, you may mention your beliefs 'en passant', and visit a Chinese place of worship.

EXAMPLE

Chinese friends and colleagues asked me about Christianity; and were disappointed that they could not attend my church, not realising that it was forbidden. When I declared Good Friday a non-working day, one Chinese colleague wanted to 'convert' on the spot – a modern day example of a 'rice Christian'!

It was, therefore, a frustration for some members of the foreign Christian community in Beijing when – in 1998 – the then visiting US President chose to attend a Chinese church rather than one of the English-speaking international churches.

◆ **Superstitions**
Unlike other commentators, I found little evidence of belief in superstitions in urban business circles beyond those traditionally associated with exchanging gifts, described in Chapter 4. The only exception was my middle-aged Chinese No 2, from Hong Kong, who applied his knowledge of Feng Shui to office layouts.

Safe subjects

As elsewhere in the world, subjects safe to discuss with the Chinese include (in alphabetical order):

◆ books (non-political), clothes, cooking, customs and traditions, entertainment (TV, films, music), family, festivals and holidays, folk-arts, home-town, grandchildren, hobbies (especially stamp collecting), jobs and careers, landscapes, music, sport, tourist attractions, weather.

Missing from this list are **pets**, which are favoured by Westerners but urban Chinese tend not to have.

On the other hand, however, the Chinese have no qualms about asking such **personal questions** as: 'How much do you earn? How old are you? Why are you unmarried? Don't you have a child?' If you are embarrassed, follow their example, mentioned below, of using humour to find a mutually face-saving way out of not answering, such as: 'Not enough! Stopped counting! Still looking! Got my hands full already!', respectively. On no account should you react in any way that suggests that they have committed a cultural gaffe, since this would cause them a loss of 'face'.

FORMS OF ADDRESS

Addressing Chinese with sufficient respect (which you can never over-do) is a complicated matter, on which you should seek guidance from – say – your Chinese advisor before meeting someone new.

Meanwhile, I recommend these guidelines for addressing the Chinese:

1. Find out how to address someone before you meet them for the first time.

2. Chinese are rarely addressed by their first names, except by family or intimate long-time friends (and sometimes close colleagues – for example: in a foreign company in China). To do so may imply that you not only have known the person since a child but also still remember them as such. Otherwise, it may be misconstrued as treating them like a child and, hence, a lack of respect.

3. Address a Chinese person by their surname (which comes first – as in: *Jiang* Zemin) preceded by a:
   – title like 'Mister', 'Madam'
   – rank like 'Director', 'Minister'.

4. Alternatively, you may just address someone by their rank; as elsewhere, dropping the 'vice' or 'deputy' prefix, thus giving them 'face'.

5. At subsequent meetings, you may precede a man's surname with the word:
   – *xiao* ('young') – if under 40 or much younger than you
   – *lao* ('old') – if over 40 or several years older than you.

6. The Chinese may reciprocate by addressing foreigners by their surname followed by *xiansheng* ('Mister') or *nüshi* ('Madam').

7. The most respectful way to address a man is by his surname followed by *lao*, equivalent to 'venerable' – for example: *Jiang lao*.

8. The most deferential way to address anyone is in the third person, rather than as 'you' – for example: 'What does the Professor think?'

9. Say *ni hao?* ('how are you?') or, more politely, *nin hao?* (where *nin* is equivalent to the French 'vous').

10. Limit physical greetings to brief single handshakes – avoid kissing, back-slapping or bear-hugging.

EXAMPLE

On arrival at Shanghai Finance College for my installation as a Guest Professor, I felt very honoured to be greeted as 'professor' and in the third person by a member of faculty.

NON-VERBAL COMMUNICATION

In addition to the relevant examples and case studies included elsewhere in this book, in order not to offend the Chinese you should observe these guidelines for non-verbal communication:

◆ **Body language**
   – always maintain proper posture
   – never (for example): slouch in easy chairs, rest your feet on a table or even shrug your shoulders
   – always use your hands to point to or manipulate something

  - never use any other part of your body (such as your feet) to point to or manipulate something
  - always signal someone by extending your hand, palm downwards, and waving it up and down
  - never point at anybody.

◆ **Eye contact and staring**
  - do not take offence if the Chinese avoid your gaze, which is how they deal with shyness or embarrassment and which you should not mistake for insincerity
  - similarly, do not overdo your eye contact with the Chinese, as they may misinterpret your behaviour as threatening or aggressive
  - conversely, do not take offence if the Chinese stare at you: normally (but not always) they mean no harm nor disrespect.

◆ **Laughter**
  - do not take offence if the Chinese react to your mishaps by laughing, which is how they hide discomfort and which you should not mistake for amusement.

◆ **Nods and grunts**
  The Chinese often signal their interlocutors with nods or verbal interjections to show they are following and understand what is being said
  - do not interpret such signals as necessarily indicating agreement.

◆ **Physical contact**
  - do not touch Chinese strangers of the opposite sex, or advanced age or high rank beyond shaking hands
  - do not indulge in any public display of affection with Chinese or foreign friends of the opposite sex beyond holding hands
  - do not take offence at light physical contact by a Chinese person of the same sex (e.g. guiding you through a door).

◆ **Silence**
  The Chinese are more comfortable than Westerners with silence, which they:
  - consider a virtue
  - use as sign of polite attention meaning 'please carry on speaking'
  - exploit as a ploy to ferret out information (by making you say

anything just to break the silence).

Moreover: what the Chinese do not say can be as important as what they do.

♦ **Smiling**
- do not take offence if the Chinese fail to smile when meeting you, which is due to being conditioned to control their feelings in public, as explained below. You should not mistake this for annoyance or unfriendliness.
- nevertheless, do not assume that a smile is always a sign of friendliness, since it could be a decoy for embarrassment or anger.

GENERAL BEHAVIOUR

In addition to the relevant examples and case studies included elsewhere in this book, in order not to offend the Chinese you should observe these guidelines for general behaviour:

♦ **Emotions**
In accordance with Confucius' teaching, the Chinese are conditioned to control their emotions to such an extent that Westerners consider them inscrutable – for which reason, you too should:
- never give way to your emotions and feelings, or otherwise behave in too carefree a manner, in public
- always respect the Confucian value of harmony
- never, but never lose your temper.

However: you may say how you feel in an objective and firm but fair and friendly manner.

♦ **Formality**
Do not take offence if, in the early stages of a new relationship, the Chinese treat you very formally, which is their way of showing respect for hierarchy, explained above, and which you should not mistake for a lack of warmth or friendliness. However: as the relationship develops, the Chinese will 'loosen up' gradually.

POSTSCRIPT

After visiting China (in 1979), Carl Rogers – the eminent psychotherapist – came to the conclusion that the Chinese discount personal feelings and emotions (Groups in Two Cultures in *Personnel and Guidance Journal*, No 58, 1979):

'I came away with the feeling that **the Chinese people are somehow fundamentally different, that their reactions are not the same as ours**. I despaired of really perceiving the world as it appears to a Chinese person. I hypothesized that with their lack of introspection they were truly unaware of their experiencing. Of course **they experience fright, or anger at times, or love, but they seemed astonishingly unaware of having these feelings**.'

(Quoted by Nancy Bragard in *Self-Disclosure as a therapeutic technique in Eastern and Western cultures*.)

What a challenge to the foreigner wishing to work more effectively with the Chinese! Hopefully, this book may help you better understand, anticipate and deal with such reactions and feelings.

APPLICATION

The following behaviours are specifically referred to again in subsequent chapters, as follows:

Topic	See chapter
Building *guanxi*	10
Business hierarchy	5, 6, 10
Changing your mind	10
Chinese politics	9
Collectivism	4, 5, 10
Conflict management	5, 10
Connections (*guanxi*)	4, 5, 6, 7, 8, 9, 10
Consensus	5, 6, 8, 10
Dead men's shoes	10
Deferring to authority	10
Disciplining staff	10
Exercising authority	10
'Face' (*mianzi*)	2, 4, 5, 6, 7, 10
'Face' by proxy	10
Forms of address	6
Forms of *guanxi*	4
General behaviour	5, 6, 7

General behaviour: emotions	5
Giving 'face'	5, 10
Harmony	10
Hierarchism	10
Laobanism	10
Levels of *guanxi*	5
Losing and saving 'face'	5, 10
Making mistakes	5, 10
Modesty and humility (*keqi*)	2, 4, 5, 6, 7, 8, 10
Non-verbal communication	5, 6
Practice of *guanxi*	5, 10
Saying 'no'	5, 6
Ritual behaviour	5
Taboo subjects	7
Whose 'face' is it anyway?	10

4

Exchanging Gifts and Favours

This Chapter details the protocol for exchanging gifts & favours between the Chinese and foreigners.

UNDERPINNING INFLUENCES AND BEHAVIOURS FOR EXCHANGING GIFTS AND FAVOURS

Correct observance is based on the following underpinning influences and behaviours:

Influence or Behaviour	See chapter
Collectivism	3
Connections (*guanxi*)	3
Corruption	1
Face (*mianzi*)	3
Forms of *guanxi*	3
Golden rule of Confucianism: reciprocity (*shu*)	1
Key concepts of Confucianism: generosity (*ren*)	1
Modesty and humility (*keqi*)	3

Of these, what most matters here is **generosity**, commended by Confucius (*Analects 17*):

'Tsze-chang asked Confucius about perfect virtue. Confucius said:

"To be able to practice five things everywhere under heaven constitutes perfect virtue."

'He begged to ask what they were, and was told:

"Gravity, **generosity of soul**, sincerity, earnestness, and kindness. If you are grave, you will not be treated with disrespect. **If you are generous, you will win all**. If you are sincere, people will repose trust in you. If you are earnest, you will accomplish much. If you are kind, this will enable you to employ the services of others" '.

Reasons for exchanging gifts

Generosity takes many forms, of which two of the most obvious and tangible are: giving presents and doing favours – or rather **exchanging** the same, following Confucius' golden rule of reciprocity and in the spirit of the Chinese proverb that: '**courtesy demands reciprocity**', explained below.

Moreover, it is not the gift that counts, but the act of giving, according to the Chinese saying that: '**the gift is nothing much, but it's the thought that counts**' (*li qing; ren yi zhong*) – which is inspired by the following Chinese legend:

Once upon a time, a man went to visit a friend, taking a swan as a gift. On the way, the swan escaped; and the man, in trying to catch it, only managed to grab a feather. Rather than return home, he continued his journey with the feather. On receiving this unexpected gift, his friend was deeply moved by the story and the man's sincerity.

Business is no exception: hence, an integral part of the Chinese business scene (at home and abroad) is **exchanging gifts**, for any of the following reasons:

1. Souvenirs to mark occasions.
2. Gratuities to show esteem or gratitude.
3. Payoffs to discharge obligations or accompany requests for favours.

Their common purpose is to build *guanxi*, for which reason giving gifts is not a 'one-off', but should be repeated from time to time.

Bribes

Gifts should never be taken or given as bribes.

In order, therefore, to avoid the recipient mistaking your gift for a bribe, you should stress your good intentions or gratitude, not the value of the gift – for which reason, when presenting a gift, you might say something like: 'I have been **truly overwhelmed** by your **extremely valuable** help and **generous** hospitality; and would **very much** like you to accept this **small** token of my **sincere appreciation** and **heartfelt thanks**.'

Whilst this might seem so obsequious as to make Uriah Heap look like an amateur, it follows the Chinese tradition of ritual humility.

Similarly: to give a very valuable gift to a powerful individual, especially in private, is still highly risky for both the giver and recipient, despite stories to the contrary – namely:

According to the US Department of Commerce (*Country Commercial Guide: China*, www.usatrade.gov, 2002):

> 'Offering and receiving **bribes** are both crimes under Chinese law, but it is unclear if giving a bribe to a foreign official in another country is a crime...Based on surveys reported in the Western media and views expressed by foreign business people and lawyers in China, it is clear that U.S. firms consider corruption in China a hindrance to foreign direct investment...'

> 'The 1979 Organic Law of the People's Courts of the PRC authorised the establishment of economic courts' with jurisdiction, inter alia, over 'various economic crimes including theft, **bribery**, and tax evasion. In 1994, the lowest level of provincial courts started to try economic cases involving foreign parties. Foreign lawyers cannot act as attorneys in Chinese courts, but may observe proceedings informally.'

CHOOSING GIFTS

Although, as explained above, 'it's the thought that counts', it is still important to select appropriate gifts and avoid inappropriate ones – particularly as giving the wrong gift to somebody you have not met before could cause offence.

Unsuitable gifts

♦ **Black and white**

Black and white colours denote death and sorrow and – whilst acceptable as a background colour – should never be the dominant colour (e.g. all-white wrapping paper or ribbon).

♦ **Cameras**
Cameras may need to be declared in writing on arrival in China, and may need to be shown again on departure (which could cause problems if they had been given away).

♦ **Clocks**
In Chinese, 'to give a clock' (*song zhong*) sounds like 'to pay one's last respects' (*songzhong*). Hence, some Chinese are very superstitious about exchanging clocks as a homonym for attending their funeral. However, not everyone in China shares this superstition.

EXAMPLES

I received a:

1. desk-clock from HSBC at the opening of its new Beijing branch

2. wrist-watch from the British Chamber of Commerce in China at the banquet to launch the Britain in China campaign

3. travel alarm-clock from flying business-class with Air China.

Nevertheless, clocks are best avoided.

♦ **Cut flowers**
Similarly, cut flowers are reminiscent of funerals and should be avoided.

♦ **Fours**
Although even numbers are lucky in China, 'four' (*si*) reads like 'death' (*si*) in Chinese, and should, therefore, be avoided.

♦ **Electric goods**
Importing too many electrical and electronic goods into China might arouse the suspicion of the Chinese Customs officials.

♦ **Excessive value**
In accordance with the Chinese proverb, quoted above, that 'courtesy demands reciprocity', the recipient is similarly obligated to the giver. Thus, to give someone such an expensive gift that they

cannot afford to reciprocate in like manner is to cause the recipient a loss of 'face'.

◆ **Green hats**
In Chinese, a man who 'wears a green hat' is a euphemism for a cuckold.

◆ **Money**
To give money – even for a Chinese host's child – would be at best a crude insult, and at worst misconstrued as an attempt at bribery and corruption.

◆ **Odd numbers**
Contrary to Western tradition, odd numbers are considered unlucky – for which reason, wedding gifts and birthday gifts for the aged are always sent in pairs, following the old Chinese saying that 'blessings come in pairs'.

◆ **Pears**
In Chinese, a 'pear' is a homophone of 'separation' and should therefore be avoided.

◆ **Tie pins, slides and cuff links**
In the days of the Mao jacket, tie pins, tie slides and cuff links were not appropriate. Today, however, with senior Chinese officials wearing Western dress more and more, such gifts are now quite acceptable.

EXAMPLE

I received all of these at various banquets hosted in Beijing by foreign companies to celebrate the opening of their Representative Offices in China.

Suitable gifts

Goods imported from the home country have prestige value and help win points in the 'face' game.

EXAMPLES

I found that the following were much appreciated:

1. **crystal** (e.g. Waterford) fruit-bowls
2. **porcelain** (e.g. Wedgwood) wall-plates.

Although Western *objets d'art* are acceptable, they may turn out to be expensive white elephants, since the Chinese may not appreciate their artistic merit (not to mention the cost) – and are, therefore, best avoided.

Collective gifts

Visitors are expected to give presents to their hosts. In theory, the acceptable practice is for the visitors to present one large collective gift to the host organisation, rather than several small gifts to individual members. In this way, not only are the Chinese socialist principles of equality and collectivism satisfied, but also the risk of personal corruption (of the recipient) and bribery (by the giver) is avoided.

Individual gifts

In practice, however, it is now customary (instead of or in addition to a collective gift) for foreigners to give small individual gifts to members of a Chinese host organisation, who are allowed to keep them provided they are of nominal value.

In this regard, I suggest that the ideal individual gift for a Chinese official should be:

♦ **Tasteful**
♦ **Modest value** (say, not exceeding RMB 200, equivalent to US$25 or £15)
♦ **Useful**
♦ **Small** enough to carry without too much trouble

(See also: Appendix 4.1)

Many **branded company mementoes** fall into this category, such as:

♦ baseball caps (other than green!), desk sets, calendars, cigarette cases, cuff-links, diaries, lapel pins, lighters, mugs, name card holders, paper-weights, pens, pocket calculators, pocket knives, tape measures, tie pins/slides, ties and tote bags.

EXAMPLES

1. The NT's tour of China with *Othello* was marked by the gift of commemorative leather bookmarks.

2. At the Centenary Roadshow in Beijing of the Chartered Insurance Institute (CII), Institute ties and Lloyd's of London document cases were gifted.

3. I commissioned several hundred locally-made leather-and-brass photograph frames (about 12 x 18 cms) with the company logo in English and Chinese, and containing a coloured picture of the company's UK head office.

For **very senior individuals** whom you know well, suitable gifts might reflect their personal interests, such as:

♦ books (illustrated, or relevant technical texts, dedicated by your CEO), cassettes or CDs, cigarettes, liqueur, perfume, and stamps or coins (mounted) – all from the home country.

EXAMPLE

I gave a set of company-branded golf-balls to a golf-playing Chinese official.

Individual gifts should correlate to the recipients' status – for which reason, from my experience, I suggest the following guidelines for giving individual gifts:

♦ **Do...**
  – carry a range of gifts, and in excess of the number of people that you expect to meet, just in case the Chinese delegation is larger and/or its members more or less senior than anticipated
  – ensure that more senior individuals receive better gifts than their junior colleagues.

♦ **Do not ...**
  – leave anybody out, not even the driver: a company brochure is
    better than nothing.

Unusual gifts

EXAMPLES

In my experience, the most unusual gift presented:
1. **to the Chinese** was: a pair of spectacles worn by a theatrical knight given to the Chinese hosts by the NT when touring China with *Othello*
2. **by the Chinese** was: a complete set of investment regulations, in Mandarin, given to me by the China Securities Regulatory Commission (CSRC).

Children

One way to melt someone's heart is to give a small gift to their child, and the Chinese are no exception.

EXAMPLE		
My teenage son received:		
What?	**From whom?**	**When?**
playing cards	colleague	before arriving in China
inflatable Santa Claus	driver	at Christmas
model boat	maid	on returning to school in the UK after the Christmas holiday

RECIPROCITY

In the spirit of the Chinese proverb, quoted above, that 'courtesy demands reciprocity', I suggest the following guidelines for exchanging gifts and favours:

♦ **Do...**
  – ensure that gifts given in return for gifts or favours roughly correlate with the magnitude of the gift or favour received, so as not to cause a loss of 'face'

- keep a balance, over time, between gifts and favours received and given
- before a **banquet** – when it is common for both sides to exchange gifts – let the Chinese know of your gift, to avoid the embarrassment of their coming empty-handed and being unable to reciprocate
- be wary of the expensive gift that precedes a request for a **favour**. With apologies to Virgil: 'Beware of Chinese bearing gifts'.

◆ **Do not...**
   - extend a light-hearted invitation to look you up next time the Chinese are in your home country. As one European business-man once found: you may be taken literally; and one day faced with an unexpected airfare and hotel bill for a mini-delegation out of the blue!
   - accept a gift from someone for whom you have never done, and do not intend to do, a favour. To save the giver's face: decline the gift politely (e.g. citing your company's policy on accepting gifts; or the airline's luggage allowance).

ETIQUETTE FOR EXCHANGING GIFTS

In China, gift-giving is an essential ingredient of courteous behaviour, with its own etiquette. The following are suggested guidelines for presenting and refusing gifts:

◆ **Wrapping and presenting**
   - **wrap** gifts in preferably red paper, cloth or a special presentation box; otherwise any other colour – except black or white – with a red ribbon
   - **present** gifts with a slight bow (by nodding your head, not bending at the waist) and both hands as a sign of respect and courtesy.

◆ **Accepting**
   In keeping with their tradition of public displays of modesty, the Chinese often make as many as three obligatory **ritual refusal gestures** when offered gifts, to avoid accusations of personal material gain – for which reason:

– do not **retract a gift** unless you sense genuine reluctance (e.g. firm and/or more than three refusals)
– do not **reject unwanted gifts** (unless unwelcome, as intimated above), but accept with a smile and thanks: you can always give them to someone else (the Chinese do!).

◆ **Opening**
In accordance with the Chinese view that the thought counts more than the gift, as explained above:
– do not **open gifts** in the presence of the giver, since to do so would draw attention to the gift and detract from the thought
– open **individual gifts** in private – a practice that also saves your 'face' by not having to feign drooling over unwanted kitsch.

Exceptionally, however, you may ask the Chinese to open your **collective gift** to them in public, explaining that this is a Western custom (which is now becoming more widespread in China).

◆ **Timing**
– at a banquet:
leave **individual gifts** at the place settings before the banquet begins
present any **collective gifts** publicly and formally at an appropriate moment (e.g. coinciding with a toast)
– at a meeting:
present all gifts at the end
first: any **collective gifts**, with much ceremony and many fine words
then: **individual gifts**, in a more low-key manner.

GUIDELINES FOR REWARDING PERSONAL SERVICE
On occasions, you may wish to reward service personnel or your Chinese staff for outstanding personal service.

Tipping
In theory, tipping is officially forbidden in socialist China (where all are equal) as a patronising and exploitative act of a capitalist regime. Selfless service to the socialist motherland, not cash, should be

sufficient motivation and reward for serving customers – which explains why customer service is at best indifferent, and occasionally blatantly rude.

EXAMPLE

When shopping in a large State-owned department store, I was told in no uncertain terms to go elsewhere if I did not like their range of goods.

In practice, however, local attitudes may change according to the moment and be at odds with government policy. Cash, not patriotism, buys goods. Thus, service personnel in many high-class places frequented by foreigners now explicitly seek tips, with an implicit alternative of poor service:

Where appropriate, I suggest these guidelines for rewarding outstanding service.

♦ **Do...**
  - consult your Chinese mentor
  - act discreetly and in private, to avoid putting the recipient in danger of being reported for, and/or accused of, flaunting the rules for personal gain
  - choose something small (not necessarily cash) that can be easily hidden in the recipient's pocket.

♦ **Do not...**
  - act in front of other people
  - give what may seem to you a paltry gift or amount, but to the recipient could represent several days' wages.

EXAMPLE

In 1998: on both occasions when I moved house, using the same international relocation company, the supervisor was very happy to accept a pot of cash to share amongst the team-members (from memory: RMB 50 each, equivalent to £4/US$6).

As with other gifts, refusal is part of the acceptance ritual, described above, which you will be expected to follow. If necessary, slip the tip into the recipient's pocket. However, given government policy, do not persist if the **refusal** seems genuine, but trust the recipient's instinct for the risk involved.

EXAMPLE

When I bought a bicycle from a large State-owned department store, a mechanic was despatched to my house (over an hour's journey) at the weekend to service it. After consulting a Chinese colleague, I tried to reward the mechanic first in cash (from memory: RMB 20 or 30, equivalent to £2/ US$3) and then with a drink, both of which were firmly and genuinely refused.

Staff gratuties
To reward **staff members** for exceptional service, work-related items or events are acceptable.

EXAMPLES

I would always host a meal for:

1. all the staff on the successful conclusion of a major project (such as the office relocation; or each visit by group board members)

2. individual employees on special occasions (such as passing examinations)

and, as and when appropriate:

3. organise a group event (such as a picnic, barbecue, ten-pin bowling or karaoke)

4. reward individuals with a clothing allowance

5. distribute moon cakes amongst company and domestic staff at the Mid-Autumn Festival.

HELPFUL HINTS
Finally, from personal experience, I offer these tips for exchanging gifts:

1. Do not **engrave** a specific gift for a specific individual, just in case you never actually get to meet that person. Rather, engrave a separate plaque that can be subsequently attached to the gift: otherwise, you cannot give the gift to anyone else.

2. Keep a **record** of gifts and favours exchanged and refused, in order to monitor the balance and avoid repetitions.

3. **When in doubt, consult your Chinese advisors**, for whom – infuriatingly – choosing the right gifts may be the most important task in planning a delegation, meeting, banquet or similar event.

APPLICATION

All the foregoing protocols are specifically referred to again in subsequent chapters, as follows:

Protocol	See chapter
Exchanging gifts and favours	5, 6, 7, 8
Staff gratuities	10

5
Negotiating Techniques

This chapter:

♦ **Outlines** the protocol and suggests tactics for negotiations between the Chinese and foreigners – the correct observance of which should improve the chances of the latter securing a successful outcome.

♦ **Assumes** a basic knowledge and understanding of negotiating techniques in general, onto which such specific protocol and tactics may be grafted.

♦ **Concentrates**, therefore, purely on the aspects peculiar to China.

Whilst the degree of formality may vary – according to the nature and importance of the occasion and relationship between the individuals involved – the underpinning influences, behaviours and protocols are the same.

Influence, behaviour or protocol	See chapter
Attitude to foreigners	2
Business hierarchy	3
Business meetings	6
Collectivism	3
Conflict management	3
Connections (*guanxi*)	3
Consensus	3

Exchanging gifts and favours	4
Face (*mianzi*)	3
General behaviour	3
Legal Environment	1
Long-term commitment	1
Modesty and humility (*keqi*)	3
Non-verbal communication	3
Note-taking	6 and 7
Open door policy	1
Relations with the West	2
Ritual behaviour	3
Saying 'no'	3
The Opium Wars and Unequal Treaties	2
The Superior Man	1

Of these, the key is *guanxi*: remember, as stated earlier, that the Chinese may set greater store by building a working relationship with you than crossing every 'T' and dotting every 'I' of an agreement. For the Chinese, personal trust is more important than paper-based contractual terms.

Caveat
I can neither guarantee the success nor be held responsible for the failure of the protocols and techniques described in this chapter.

Apology and acknowledgement
I have so often used and recommended – and hence been influenced by – Scott Seligman's excellent book *Dealing with the Chinese* (see bibliography) during my China workshops at Farnham Castle International Briefing and Conference Centre that I hope I may be forgiven for following a similar approach, especially in the structure and choice of headings, without intentionally cloning its content as my own.

Rather, I have genuinely attempted to present my own views – in my own words and based on my own experience – albeit under Seligman's headings which I have tried to use merely as 'springboards'.

Examples
The protocols and techniques described below are illustrated with only a few examples, since they are followed by a comprehensive case study.

PREPARING FOR AND CONDUCTING NEGOTIATIONS
Preparing for and conducting negotiations is really no different from any other business meeting except in one respect:

Your negotiating team should have the following:

Composition	Characteristics
◆ bi-lingual note-taker	◆ a few grey hairs
◆ China business expert	◆ conciliatory
◆ China legal expert	◆ culturally aware (non-jingoistic/ non-xenophobic)
◆ experienced negotiator	
◆ financial expert	◆ equanimous
◆ interpreter	◆ impervious to flattery
◆ senior empowered decision-maker	◆ patient
◆ subject-matter technical expert	

These lists are deliberately in alphabetical order, rather than of priority, since:

◆ the **roles** are not mutually exclusive: the same person may fill several, or vice-versa

◆ not everyone may possess all the **characteristics**, although jointly the team should.

CHINESE NEGOTIATING TACTICS
When dealing with them, you might find that Chinese negotiators may try to...

1. control the arrangements
2. exploit your and their weaknesses
3. exploit your remorse
4. trip you up
5. embarrass you
6. play you off against your competitors
7. approach you via a third party
8. pretend to be annoyed with you
9. go over old ground with you
10. quote their law at you
11. manage your expectations

as detailed below.

The extent and manner to which any tactic or response is used or appropriate, respectively, may depend on whether the negotiations are:

♦ **unilateral**: only one party is trying to buy or sell

♦ **bilateral**: both parties are interested in buying and selling or working in a government-to-government partnership.

In the latter case, negotiations are more likely to be conducted by the Chinese as between equals in a symmetrical manner (that is: with as much give as take).

Responding to Chinese tactics
Most of the negotiating tactics that the Chinese might employ may:

♦ involve '**face**'
♦ be countered by your:
  – playing the Chinese at their own game
  – not rising to the bait.

I suggest the following guidelines for responding to Chinese negotiators:

1. If they try to control the arrangements
Traditionally, the Chinese prefer to conduct and host negotiations with foreigners in China, in an attempt to cast them in a supplicatory role and thereby make them feel subservient.

Besides costing the foreigners time and money, the Chinese can play for time.

Note: Nevertheless: being physically close to the real decision-makers with whom the Chinese negotiators will necessarily have to consult may speed up the process. This is because it is neither usual nor the done thing for the former to attend detailed discussions; but rather appear only at the very end, when all is agreed – such as: for the final banquet and official '**signing ceremony**'.

How the Chinese may try to do it
a) Quibble over minor details in the initial stages and then cram all the important points into the final stages.

b) Delay proceedings and/or take time out, ostensibly to confer in private.

c) Never leave you alone.

What the Chinese may hope to achieve
a) Coerce you into compromising – out of sheer desperation to reach some form of agreement before returning home, rather than none at all.

b) Test your bottom line under pressure.

c) Make you think that you have upset them, and thereby force you to reveal your bottom-line concessions in an attempt to save your '**face**'.

How you should respond
a) **Play the Chinese at their own game** by insisting that some of the negotiations take place in your home country.

b) Tell the Chinese your timetable *ab initio*, and stick to it (unless you really have to reach agreement before returning home).

2. If they try to exploit your and their weaknesses
The Chinese may try to discover and exploit your 'Achilles' heel' as well as reveal and exploit their own.

How the Chinese may try to do it
a) Play on your personal and corporate fear of failing to reach agreement.

b) Contrast China's 'poverty' and lack of commercial experience with your company's wealth and experience.

c) Flatter you.

What the Chinese may hope to achieve
Persuade you to concede terms that you would otherwise not accept, out of desperation and/or to save your '**face**' by reaching some form of agreement before returning home, rather than none at all.

How you should respond
a) Resist taking the bait: **if they see that you are impervious to such tactics, the Chinese may desist**.

b) If you really have to reach agreement before returning home, do not let the Chinese know.

3. If they try to exploit your remorse
The decline and fall of the Chinese Empire, and thus of China's preeminence in the world, is in no small wise due to the incursions of and invasions by foreign powers during the second half of the nineteenth and first half of the twentieth centuries (see Chapter 2).

How the Chinese may try to do it
Remind you of any damage done to China by your country.

What the Chinese may hope to achieve
Persuade you to 'make amends' by conceding terms that you might otherwise not accept, in order to save the '**face**' of your country.

How you should respond
a) Refuse to discuss, and disassociate yourself from, such issues: **if they see that you are impervious to such tactics, the Chinese may desist**.

b) Insist on 'sticking to the point'.

4. If they try to trip you up
The Chinese are inveterate note-takers.

How the Chinese may try to do it
a) Quote back at you something you and/or your colleague(s) once said and/or agreed, on and/or off the record, in- and/or outside the negotiating room.

b) Equally: forget something they and/or their colleague(s) once said and/or agreed, on and/or off the record, in- and/or outside the negotiating room.

What the Chinese may hope to achieve
Persuade you to concede to their terms, by honouring what you and/or your colleague(s) said and/or agreed on an earlier occasion – depending on whether it supports or conflicts with your present stance – in order to save your '**face**'.

How you should respond
a) **Play the Chinese at their own game** by keeping your own detailed notes, in order to 'retaliate'.

b) Never speak off the record.

c) Avoid talking business outside the negotiating room.

5. If they try to embarrass you
The Chinese lay great emphasis on formal courtesy, as manifested in their observance of ritual etiquette, from which business is not exempt.

How the Chinese may try to do it
Accuse you on a trumped-up charge of:

a) breaking the 'ground rules' that you agreed at the outset

b) unfriendly behaviour

c) being devious.

What the Chinese may hope to achieve
a) Fool you into thinking that you have genuinely offended them; and thus. . .

b) Persuade you to 'make amends' by conceding terms that you would otherwise not accept, in order to save your '**face**'

How you should respond
a) Remember that the accusations are probably a ploy rather than genuine.

b) Keep your own detailed notes, in order to refute accusations of being devious.

c) Resist taking the bait: **if they see that you are impervious to such tactics, the Chinese may desist**.

6. If they try to play you off against your competitors
Besides genuine competition, the Chinese are not averse to 'inventing' fictitious competitors.

How the Chinese may try to do it
Either:
a)   Imply that:
    – you are less generous and/or co-operative
    – your products and/or services are more attractive than the competition.

Or:
b) Imply that they are not negotiating (any longer) with your competitors.

c) Share your competitors' 'secrets' with you.

What the Chinese may hope to achieve
Either:
a) Persuade you to equal or better the competition's terms which you would otherwise not accept, out of sheer desperation to reach some form of agreement before returning home, rather than none at all.

b) Test your bottom line under pressure.

Or:
c) Coax from you genuinely confidential information, by lulling you into a false sense of security.

How you should respond
a) Know your competitors; and play to your strengths (even by contrasting these with your competitors' weaknesses, if your corporate culture so allows).

b) Resist taking the bait: **if they see that you are impervious to such tactics, the Chinese may desist**.

7. If they approach you via a third party
The Chinese may use third parties to convey delicate messages or 'test the waters'.

What the Chinese may hope to achieve
Save their own '**face**' if the intermediary fails, by denying (s)he was
authorised to act on their behalf.

How you should respond
Play the Chinese at their own game by using a go-between yourself.

8. If they try to pretend to be annoyed with you
In theory: following Confucius' teaching that the 'Superior Man'
should not lose his temper – the Chinese disapprove of outbursts of
anger.

In practice: they are not averse to affecting anger if it will help them
get their own way.

How the Chinese may try to do it
Accuse you of some trumped-up charge.

What the Chinese may hope to achieve
a) Fool you into thinking that you have genuinely offended them; and
    thus...

b) Persuade you to make amends by conceding terms that you would
    otherwise not accept, in order to save your '**face**'.

c) Find a '**face** saving' pretence to de-rail the negotiations.

How you should respond
a) Remember that the accusations are probably a ploy rather than
    genuine.

b) Resist taking the bait: **if they see that you are impervious to such
    tactics, the Chinese may desist**.

c) **Play the Chinese at their own game**.

9. If they try to go over old ground with you
Following the adage 'If at first you don't succeed: try, try again', the
Chinese may continue to raise the same issues until the very last
minute, even as they are saying goodbye.

How the Chinese may try to do it
Raise an issue that was apparently resolved earlier (in your favour),
but as if it were not.

What the Chinese may hope to achieve

a) Fool you into thinking that the issue was not resolved; and thus...

b) Persuade you to concede terms that you would otherwise not accept, out of desperation and/or to save your '**face**' by reaching some form of agreement before returning home, rather than none at all.

How you should respond

a) Keep your own detailed notes, in order to remind the Chinese of what was agreed and when.

b) Refuse to discuss the issue.

c) **Play the Chinese at their own game** by agreeing to discuss the issue again so long as they will reconsider an issue previously resolved in their favour.

10. If they try to quote their law at you

The Chinese may assume they are more familiar than you with their commercial law; and exploit your ignorance of the same to justify anything they want and you do not and vice-versa.

How the Chinese may try to do it

a) Quote (allegedly) unpublished commercial codes.

b) Say that their superiors may only accept certain contractual terms (e.g. standard wordings).

What the Chinese may hope to achieve

Fool you into conceding terms that you would otherwise not accept, to save your '**face**' (i.e. hide your ignorance).

How you should respond

a) Retain a legal expert.

b) Obtain copies of the Chinese commercial codes.

c) **Play the Chinese at their own game** by telling them your superiors may never accept certain contractual terms.

11. If they try to manage your expectations

Either raise your expectations or lower your expectations.

What the Chinese may hope to achieve

Either persuade you to concede terms that you would otherwise not accept, through fear of losing an apparent done-deal at the last moment.

Or:

a) Hide their inability to deliver as much as you had originally hoped.

b) Increase your gratitude for whatever crumbs eventually fall from the Chinese table.

DOS AND DON'TS FOR NEGOTIATING WITH THE CHINESE

Here are some guidelines for negotiating with the Chinese:

Do...

♦ prepare beforehand
♦ remember that the final decision(s) may be made by persons not at the meeting(s)
♦ inflate your price
♦ play to the Chinese strengths
♦ look for opportunities to empathise with the Chinese
♦ display long-term commitment to China
♦ go over every detail of the contract
♦ be prepared for much back-tracking, repetition, ambiguity and inevitable misunderstandings
♦ take detailed notes
♦ be able to walk away from the table
♦ know where the exits are
♦ control your emotions
♦ check your ego at the door
♦ be careful what you say to the media.

Do not
♦ try to resolve problems individually
♦ concede too easily
♦ hesitate to cut your losses
♦ reject a Chinese position out of hand
♦ assume that the Chinese may make decisions for economic reasons alone

- assume there is such a thing as 'China plc'
- speak off the record
- lose your temper
- lose your patience
- embarrass the Chinese
- gloat at a successful agreement

as detailed below.

Do
When negotiating with the Chinese, do...

Prepare beforehand
How   You must ensure that you gain immediate access to the key Chinese negotiators.
See also pages 126–132.

Why   Otherwise you may subsequently need to be referred to higher-level officials – who may disregard any agreements you have already reached, and oblige you to start again from scratch.

Remember that final decisions may be made by persons not at the meeting(s).

How   Having gained access to the key Chinese negotiators, you should help them devise language acceptable to their key decision makers.

Why   Even if you gain immediate access to the key Chinese negotiators, any agreements you reach with them may still need to be reviewed and ratified by their superiors.

(Link to above: Chinese negotiating tactics (1) Control the arrangements.)

Inflate your price
How   Without being wholly out of line with the competition, you should inflate your price slightly and then give away a lesser amount (say 15% and 10%, respectively), so that both you and the Chinese 'win'.

Why   1. Otherwise, the Chinese may assume that your quote is flexible; and, consequently, continue to haggle until they secure some concession.

2. Such concession may also give '**face**' to the key Chinese negotiators by allowing them to report some good news to their superiors – who, in turn, may be more kindly disposed to ratifying any agreements you reach.

(Link to above: Chinese negotiating tactics (6) Play you off against your competitors.)

Play to the Chinese strengths
How   Similarly, your arguments should give '**face**' to the Chinese.

Why   The Chinese may remember, resent and retaliate against your taking advantage of their weaknesses.

Look for opportunities for empathy
How   You should be prepared to talk around a subject rather than address it directly.

Why   Some Chinese may still consider it good manners to take an indirect approach – although others may be less sensitive and more direct.

Display long-term commitment to China
How   You should never express (or allow the Chinese to sense) any doubts that you may have about the ultimate feasibility of the object of your negotiations.

Why   The Chinese may misinterpret your hesitancy as insincerity. See also Chapter 1: Open Door Policy and Chapter 9: Long Term Commitment.

(Link to above: Chinese negotiating tactics (5) Embarrass you.)

Go over every detail of the contract
How   You should ensure that you discuss all the issues, taking all the time necessary and allowed.

Why   Otherwise, the Chinese may:
1. Not fully understand the language nor, consequently, the terms and/or conditions of the contract.

2. Identify but consequently keep quiet about some ambiguity in the contract that may subsequently benefit them and/or disadvantage you.

(Link to above: Chinese negotiating tactics (9) Go over old ground.)

Be prepared for much back-tracking, repetition, ambiguity and inevitable misunderstandings

How   You should avoid 'pointing the finger' and remember that the person you rebuke today may be your JV partner tomorrow!

(Link to above: Chinese negotiating tactics (1) Control the arrangements.)

Take detailed notes

How   See also Chapter 6: Note-taking.

Why   As a consequence of the previous two 'Dos'.

(Link to above: Chinese negotiating tactics (4) Trip you up (5) Embarass you (9) Go over old ground.

Be able to walk away from the table

How   You should never put or get yourself into a position where (the Chinese sense that) you need to have an agreement.

Why   Otherwise, the Chinese may try to:
    1. Exploit your position.

    2. Push you to the verge of aborting the negotiations as a ploy for them to determine your true bottom line, or pull out without their losing '**face**', when what they may really be after is information to use as a weapon to strike a deal with a competitor.

(Link to above: Chinese negotiating tactics (2) Exploit your weaknesses.)

Know where the exits are

How   The Chinese may leave you a way out. However, they may not necessarily want you to take it.

Why   1. You should leave the Chinese an exit as a way of their saving '**face**', a sign of your trust and, consequently, a potential means of building good will. If they take it, the sooner you find out the better.

2. Leaving yourself an exit may be more tricky, because – unless they have left one for you already (see above) – the Chinese may mis-interpret it as a lack of commitment on your part.

(Link to above: Do be able to walk away from the table.)

Control your emotions
Why   The Chinese are:
1. not only conditioned to control their own emotions

2. but also reputedly able to read your emotions
   which may put you at a disadvantage in the 'poker game' of business negotiations.

Check your ego at the door
(Link to above: Chinese negotiating tactics (2) Exploit your weaknesses.)

Be careful what you say to the media
Why   The Chinese:
1. Do not publicise (i.e. leak) agreements until they are signed, sealed and delivered.

2. Dislike surprises and hate public embarrassment.

(Link to above: Chinese negotiating tactics (5) Embarrass you.)

Do not
When negotiating with the Chinese, do NOT...

Try to resolve problems individually
Instead   You should follow the Chinese example of:
1. first listening to all the problems

2. only then deciding what concessions if any you are prepared to give and always keep a couple of concessions up your sleeve, in case you need to offer them to close the deal.

Why   The Chinese may:

1. Not only be non-plussed by your zeal to please them; but also use it later to embarrass you.

2. Prove difficult to be persuaded to back-track on previous concessions – even though they may try to do the same to you.

3. Use **silence** as a negotiating tool.

(Link to above: Chinese negotiating tactics (5) Embarrass you (9) Go over old ground.)

Concede too easily

Instead   You should follow the Chinese example of not giving up anything without a fight – however unimportant to you – since you can use it to extract something from them.

Why   1. The Chinese may not give up something without a fight – however unimportant to them – since they may use it to extract something from you.

2. By conceding something unimportant easily, you may run the risk of:
   – convincing the Chinese that you do not value it
   – losing its value as a bargaining chip.

(Link to above: Chinese negotiating tactics (2) Exploit your weaknesses.)

Hesitate to cut your losses

Why   The Chinese may not be able to deliver what they promise.

(Link to above: Chinese negotiating tactics (11) Manage your expectations.)

Reject a Chinese position out of hand

Instead   You should counter any preposterous proposition by the Chinese by:

1. Drawing them into a discussion.

2. Steering them in a more constructive direction.

Why 1. A rebuff may cause the Chinese a loss of '**face**'.

    2. 'Parry' is more effective than 'thrust'.

Assume that the Chinese may make decisions for economic reasons alone

Why 1. Profit is a relatively new motivator in China.

    2. The Chinese have traditionally made decisions for political reasons.

    3. Even if the project goes 'belly up', the technology may remain in China.

Assume there is such a thing as 'China plc'

Instead You should not:

    1. Overestimate the ability of your Chinese negotiators to resolve the objections of their political rivals.

    2. Underestimate the ability of such rivals to scupper the negotiations.

Why There is no such thing as a corporate China when it comes to doing business: everyone is out for what (s)he can get for themselves or their *guanxi* circle.

Speak off the record

Instead See also: Chapter 6 Note-taking.
Why See also: Chapter 6 Note-taking.

(Link to above – Do take detailed notes.)

Lose your temper

Instead You should:

    1. Always be polite, softly spoken and gentle.

    2. Nevertheless: very occasionally, anger can be used to good effect between you and the Chinese (playing them at their own game).

Why The Chinese strongly disapprove of outbursts of anger, which they consider a sign of weakness – following the teaching of Confucius that, come what may, the 'Superior Man' should:

1. Never lose his temper, which is a loss of '**face**'.

2. Always exercise self-control.

(Link to above – Do control your emotions. Chinese negotiating tactics (8) Pretend to be annoyed with you.)

Lose your patience
Why   Joint ventures, even when all parties may appear willing, can take several years to negotiate.

(Link to above – Do control your emotions. See also – Chapter 1: Open Door Policy and Chapter 9: Long Term Commitment.)

Embarrass the Chinese
Why   You and/or the Chinese will lose 'face'.

Gloat at a successful agreement
Instead Be happy, by all means, but not triumphal.

Why   If you have 'won' then the Chinese have 'lost', which will:

1. Cause them a loss of '**face**'.

2. Earn them the opprobrium of their superiors.

OVERCOMING OBJECTIONS
Scott D. Seligman (*op. cit.*, pp. 146–8) suggests the following supplementary tactics for overcoming objections where not already included above.

1. Appeal to a higher-level decision-maker.
2. Ask the right question; push the right button.
3. Be 'Mr nice guy'.
4. Show respect; be modest.
5. Take risks.
6. Use your *guanxi* to go through the back door (*zou houmen*).

When all else fails, try the three 'Fs' – be: Firm, Fair and Friendly.

Post script
Only after writing this chapter was I able to obtain a copy of Carolyn Blackman's masterpiece *Negotiating China* (see Bibliography). Had I

done so beforehand I might not have dared attempt the subject!

Keep calm, even when someone asks you for an exorbitant favour in exchange for a promise that (s)he may not be able to deliver.

Protagonists

The four protagonists in this case study are:

Nationality	Protagonist	Relationship to others
foreign	**businessman** living in China	
Chinese	potential joint-venture or **JV partner**	*known* to the businessman and with whom he already enjoyed good and direct relations
Chinese	**intermediary**	*unknown* to the businessman or his home office; but *known* to the JV partner
foreign	**third party**, not living in China	*known* to the intermediary and businessman's home office

All have been anonymised to protect their identities. However, the facts are wholly true and genuine.

Day 1 – Tuesday
One Tuesday, the businessman received, via the third party, an unsolicited approach from the intermediary, who offered to set up a deal with the potential JV partner.

As it happened, the businessman had already arranged a meeting with the potential JV partner early on the following Monday morning (Day 5).

Day 2 – Wednesday
On the Wednesday, when the businessman checked the intermediary's credentials:

- The **intermediary** explained that he:
  - would be present at the scheduled meeting with the potential JV partner, whom he claimed to know well
  - wished to help the businessman better understand the potential JV partner's position so that both parties might reach a mutually beneficial agreement.

- The **potential JV partner** denied all knowledge of the intermediary's role.

Day 3 – Thursday

On the Thursday morning, after consulting his home office, the businessman reluctantly agreed to meet the intermediary on the following morning (Friday – Day 4), for the following reasons.

Purpose	Protagonist	Reason
placate the	potential **JV partner**	just in case the intermediary really were able to jeopardise the meeting
save the 'face' of the	**intermediary**	by not saying 'no' (which might have shut the door to further negotiation)
please the	**third party**	

At the same time, the businessman made it clear to the intermediary that he would only agree to his attending the scheduled meeting with the potential JV partner if the latter also agreed (which, at the time, they had not).

Day 4 – Friday

On the Friday morning, the meeting took place in the businessman's office.

True to Chinese negotiating tactics to try to gain the upper hand, the intermediary took along an interpreter – probably for the following reasons:

In order to. . .	Because. . .
counter the twin disadvantages of being (1) the guest and (2) not on his own territory — by 'upping the numbers' with an ally	most such meetings are normally hosted by the Chinese and on their own territory; thus...
	he expected to be outnumbered by 'hostile' people
gain 'thinking time', whilst the proceedings were being translated	most educated Chinese in his position have some command of English
advise him *sotto voce* in Chinese on how best to negotiate with foreigners	even If the intermediary did not know, the interpreter might (through his work exposing him to foreigners); and...
	the businessman was unlikely to know Chinese well enough fully to understand what was being said; thus...
	this would help save the intermediary's 'face'.

Playing the intermediary at his own game (i.e. in order to level the playing field), the businessman then also invited his Chinese bilingual personal assistant to attend — for the following reasons:

In order to. . .	Because. . .
even up the numbers	this suggested subtly to the intermediary that the businessman knew the basic 'rules of the game' and was, therefore, no 'greenhorn'
advise him *sotto voce* in English on how best to negotiate with the Chinese	the intermediary was unlikely to know English well enough fully to understand what was being said; thus...
	this would help save the businessman's 'face'
monitor the performance of the intermediary's interpreter	it was apparent from the outset that the interpreter might not have a good enough command of English correctly to translate the businessman's nuances; and... this would keep in check the interpreter's advice to the intermediary
demonstrate his seniority and re-enforce his 'face'	had the businessman not done so, the intermediary might have concluded that the former was not senior enough to warrant one and, thus, not his equal

Proposal

The preliminaries over, the intermediary claimed:

- The potential JV partner had three pet major building projects (the details of which are outside the scope of this case study).
- If the businessman were to finance just one, the potential JV partner might consider agreeing to a joint venture.
- Were another company also to finance one, the potential JV partner would have to choose between the businessman and that other company.
- Were the businessman or that other company to finance two, there would be no contest (i.e. assuming that the total value of both projects exceeded that of the remaining one).
- Were the businessman or that other company to finance all three, well then...!
- He was giving the businessman first refusal – since, having done his homework, he considered the businessman's company to be the ideal candidate for the potential JV partner.

Response

The businessman:

politely. . .	in order to. . .
listed attentively AND... took copious notes AND... used appropriate searching questions	dissemble his incredulity at the sheer scale of 'cheek' of the proposal with feigned interest, AND...
	ensure (the intermediary saw that) he accurately recorded the details of the proposal
modestly explained that he could not decide, but would have to refer to his home office (immediately)	save his own 'face'
	since the Chinese: • have made an art of public demonstrations of modesty • prefer collective over individual decision-making as a means of taking advantage of collective wisdom • do not (like to) make off the cuff decisions the intermediary would recognise this ploy as typically Chinese and thus accept it with good grace

warmly thanked the intermediary for the opportunity of first refusal for such projects	build the intermediary's 'face' in true Chinese style by expressions of flattery and gratitude (albeit false) in front of others

promised to let him have an early answer (rather than say 'no')	save his own face
	keep the door open
	since the Chinese refuse politely in a number of ways (including lying) without exactly saying 'no' in order to: ♦ save face ♦ avoid shutting the proverbial door to further renegotiation ♦ leave room for further manoeuvre the intermediary would recognise this ploy as typically Chinese and thus accept it with good grace

Outcome

After the intermediary left, the businessman's Chinese personal assistant expressed her shock that what had just happened was undoubtedly a request for a substantial bribe.

The businessman immediately reported to his home office, which agreed that he had acted wholly appropriately.

Later that afternoon, about 4 p.m., the potential JV partner's secretary telephoned the businessman's personal assistant to cancel the meeting scheduled for early the following Monday morning (Day 5), pleading a last-minute summons to a high-level governmental meeting. Such an excuse is not uncommon and frequently genuine – which, in this case, it was subsequently confirmed to be.

On informing his home office, the businessman was informed that the third party had already told them that the intermediary had complained of his lack of cooperation – a charge that the home office flatly denied.

Happy ending

Some two to three months later, the businessman invited the potential JV partner to a banquet, which they accepted.

Some 18 months later, the businessman happened to meet by chance a contemporary from school who – to cut a long story short – turned out to have been the third party! After a brief conversation, the third party retracted his view of the businessman's performance: he had no idea of the intermediary's proposal, which shocked him.

Footnote

Even if the businessman had conceded, there was no guarantee that the joint venture would have been successful. Chequebook negotiating has reputedly worked occasionally in the past; but the Chinese are reluctant to bite the hand that feeds them: in other words, while they can still dangle carrots and receive presents, why hand over the carrots?

As a Chinese university professor once said to me: why should the Chinese use their own money – of which he claimed that they had more than sufficient – while the West is prepared to hand theirs over by the barrowful?

APPLICATION

The following protocols are specifically referred to again in subsequent chapters, as follows:

Topic	See chapter
Negotiating techniques	6, 7

6
Business Meetings

This chapter details the protocol for business meetings between the Chinese and foreigners – the correct observance of which should improve the chances of the latter securing a useful meeting and successful outcome.

UNDERPINNING INFLUENCES, BEHAVIOURS AND PROTOCOLS FOR BUSINESS MEETINGS

Whilst the degree of formality may vary – according to the nature and importance of the occasion and relationship between the individuals involved – the underpinning influences, behaviours and protocols are the same.

Influence, behaviour or protocol	See chapters
Business heirarchy	3
Connections (*guanxi*)	3
Consensus	3
Education system	2
Exchanging gifts and favours	4
Face (*mianzi*)	3
Forms of address	3
General behaviour and non-verbal communication	3
Modesty and humility (*keqi*)	3
Negotiating techniques	5
Overseas Chinese (*huaqiao*)	2
Reciprocity (*shu*)	1 and 4
Relationship with and attitude to foreigners	2
Saying 'no'	3
Sexual equality and mores	2
Sexually provocative clothing	2

MAKING ARRANGEMENTS

Whatever the occasion (e.g. a courtesy call, high-level negotiations or a formal banquet), the **how**, **when** and **with whom** to make arrangements are similar, if not the same.

How

It is common, if not necessary, for **intermediaries** (individual or corporate) to arrange meetings on behalf of the parties themselves for any of the following reasons:

The parties may:

1. Not know each other, and hence need to rely on third parties whom they both know and trust (following the Chinese practice of *guanxi*).

2. Be of such seniority that it would be *infra dig*, in Chinese terms (i.e. loss of 'face'), for them to make their own arrangements.

3. Not speak each other's language, and hence need the services of someone who does.

The process may involve several levels of intermediary; and be by telephone and/or in writing.

EXAMPLE

My bilingual Chinese PA or senior English-speaking Chinese member of staff would usually arrange my meetings via the other parties' opposite numbers, whom they invariably knew directly or through a friend of a friend, using their *guanxi*. However, I used specialist consultants with impeccable political credentials to broker meetings between my international board members and Chinese government ministers.

Thus, '**cold calling**' is not appropriate in China, unless via the appropriate governmental external affairs department which acts as its own in-house intermediary.

When

Arranging meetings is a nightmare; and flexibility the solution.

Contrary to Western practice, appointments should be made later rather than earlier. The Chinese so dislike committing to future appointments (in case they cannot keep them) that they actually prefer **last-minute arrangements** when they have a clearer idea of the other calls on their time – say: not more than two weeks ahead.

Sometimes, meetings may not be **finalised** until the day before, or the day itself. This is especially frustrating when participants are attending from the home country and are already on the aeroplane; but is explained by the Chinese view that there is no urgency until they arrive in China, since anything could happen in the meantime to abort the visit.

Meetings are often **rearranged** at the last minute.

Case Study

I had arranged for my international Deputy CEO to host a banquet at 12:30 p.m. for the Director of Foreign Affairs of the CSRC; and at 4.30 p.m. to meet a Vice-Minister at MOFTEC, some 30 minutes away by car from the banquet venue.

At 1 p.m., in the middle of the banquet, the Vice-Minister's office phoned me at the banquet venue to bring forward the meeting to 2 p.m. or otherwise to cancel it.

My first reaction was indignation, but to no avail: to be fair, to placate me, the Vice-Minister's office offered the alternative of meeting at the original time but with another government official presiding of lower rank than the Vice-Minister and the Deputy CEO.

Since I and the Vice-Minister's office knew that such an alternative would be a loss of 'face' for the Deputy CEO in Chinese eyes – for reasons explained below and because the Vice-Minister outranked the CSRC Director – the meeting went ahead (on empty stomachs!).

Occasionally, meetings may be **cancelled** at the last minute, amidst much embarrassment – especially if the foreign delegation has already arrived in China – because the Chinese principal has been 'summoned' by the powers that be.

EXAMPLES

1. My boss arrived in China at mid-day for a meeting (confirmed 36 hours earlier) first thing the following morning with the Chair of a leading SOE, only to be told that they had just been invited to a week-long governmental conference.
2. Even I was caught off-guard during a visit to Shanghai in February 2003, when one of my prime appointments – made well in advance and confirmed only days earlier – was cancelled with just five minutes notice!

To protest is futile, since no one is inviolate.

EXAMPLES

In 1998, I was present at an official banquet in Beijing when the British Premier – who was the principal guest of honour – not only arrived late, because his scheduled meeting with the then Chinese President had over-run, but also had to leave early in response to a sudden and unexpected, but nevertheless welcome, invitation from the President to a further impromptu meeting.

In such ways do the Chinese put foreigners in their place, and remind them who is in charge!

With whom

In accordance with the rules of business hierarchy, meetings should take place between principals of equal rank – which means in practice that, as a general rule, the rank of the foreign and Chinese principals will determine the maximum available and minimum required rank of the Chinese and foreign counterparts, respectively.

Hence, until the details of the foreign principal are confirmed, the rank of the Chinese principal may not be made known – let alone the name. Meeting any (Vice-)Minister may be difficult; but nothing compared to meeting a specific one, which requires the cast-iron guarantee of a specific foreign principal of at least equal rank.

The **provenance** of the **foreign principal** is also important. That someone should come all the way from the UK or USA head office (even if resident in China) is a far greater sign of commitment to and respect for China than, say, from Singapore or other Asian regional office.

PREPARING FOR MEETINGS

Whatever the occasion, preparation should include **Agenda Setting** and **Briefing** – even for a banquet, where either party may take advantage of the conviviality to try to catch the other 'off guard' and negotiate new concessions or information.

Agenda setting

Chinese organisations typically request background information before they consent to formal discussions, for the following reasons:

1. The Chinese dislike surprises, preferring to hammer out their own positions in advance of a meeting in order to present a united front, in keeping with their predilection for consensus and practice of collective decision-making.

2. Similarly, they also prefer to react to others' ideas, rather than bear the onus of setting the scope of the discussions themselves.

3. Knowing what will be discussed beforehand also permits them to select the **proper participants** for a meeting. Otherwise, foreigners are likely to be fobbed off with public relations or external affairs personnel who have a liaison role, but are not decision-makers.

4. To establish **credentials** of and on both sides.

Consequently, you should provide: a **detailed agenda**, with as much information as possible about the topics you wish to discuss; and a **list of participants**, with brief career résumés – and give the Chinese time to study your request.

Likewise, ask the Chinese for similar information, if they request the meeting.

All documentation should be: bilingual; in simple language (to ease translation); and presented (if at the meeting) with both hands.

Briefing
Ensure that every member of your group – and not just the leader or others who may be called upon to speak – is fully briefed, as per the following ten-point checklist:

1. Overall key aims and objectives of the meeting; and individual contributions and roles.

2. Meeting etiquette.

3. Recent and planned developments in China (e.g. political, economic and legal).

4. Details of the Chinese organisation with whom you are meeting (e.g. structure and performance).

5. Personal details and career history of the Chinese principal and senior ranking participants.

6. Questions the Chinese participants may ask of you; and answers you may and may not give.

7. Questions that you may and may not ask of the Chinese participants.

8. Plans and achievements of your organisation, and its main competitors, in relation to China.

9. History of your organisation's previous relationship and meetings with the Chinese organisation, at home and in China.

10. What and not to say.

EXAMPLE

I used to prepare a full briefing-pack for each programme of meetings between my international board members and senior Chinese government officials (at about six-weekly intervals), including a literal transcript of an opening speech, follow-up remarks and questions, and answers to frequently asked questions (FAQs).

Otherwise, meetings can quickly resemble Daniel going into the lions' den.

EXAMPLE

Within days of arriving in China, I was invited by a Chinese colleague to pay a '**courtesy call**' on an acquaintance, a mid-ranking offical at the PBOC. What constituted 'courtesy' was never defined, and did not seem to warrant a briefing. However, meeting etiquette still had to be observed, and I was expected to deliver a speech (albeit impromptu). Afterwards, when commenting favourably on the lack of formality, I suitably admonished my Chinese colleague to brief me before all meetings, however 'informal'.

Purpose
From that courtesy call, I realised that the Chinese expect meetings to have a purpose that benefits them; otherwise, why give up their precious time? Reminiscing does not fall into that category.

Thus, the Chinese will soon stop agreeing to meet you unless they feel that: **you** have **something new** to say or offer; and **they** are gaining **new benefit** at each meeting.

Dress and jewellery
Westerners should wear Western business attire – not least because it has now been largely adopted by senior Chinese officials – according to the following guidelines:

In winter

1. Bundle up to keep warm.
2. If the meeting room is not heated you can always keep your coat on!

In summer
1. No one will expect you to wear a jacket and tie.

2. Nevertheless, make no assumptions: it is better to arrive in jacket and tie and be invited to remove them, than to dress down only to find that the Chinese have dressed up for the occasion!

Should you wear **jewellery**, be aware that:

- On the one hand: modest gold jewellery and a quality watch may gain you 'face'.

- On the other hand: the Chinese propensity for public modesty could be offended by overly 'flash' jewellery.

LOGISTICS
In planning a meeting with the Chinese, apart from the general considerations in China of **when** (i.e. timing) and **where** (i.e. venue), non-Chinese should pay special attention to the peculiar issues, in China or elsewhere, of **note-taking** and **interpreting**.

Timing
The working week is now officially 40 hours spread over five days. Thus, offices and government departments tend to be open Mondays to Fridays between about 8:30 a.m. and 5:30 p.m., with a midday lunch break of an hour or so.

As a general rule, meetings:

- should fit within these timeframes, and **finish** half-an-hour before the end of the working morning or afternoon (ie by 11:30 a.m. or 4:30 p.m. respectively).

- may last no more than one hour (and sometimes only 30 minutes with very senior and busy Government officials). As Mao said:

'Meetings should not go on too long' (13 March 1949)

- must allow for the process of **interpretation** – which reduces by a half, if not to a third, the effective discussion time.

Venue

In China, meetings are normally held in spacious, purpose-built, air-conditioned **conference rooms** rather than overcrowded, noisy and stuffy offices.

Soft chairs and/or sofas line the perimeter of the room or are arranged around a central oblong table (see p. 140). Next to the chairs are small tables for the teacups, which are constantly filled by a discreet army of flunkies.

However – in my experience – **ashtrays** and **spittoons** are rarely if ever provided or used, although many Chinese are still prone to loud and unashamed spitting in public.

Note-taking

Ensure that your group includes a **bilingual note-taker** (with the permission of the principal Chinese participant), for the following reasons:

1. The Chinese are inveterate note-takers – for which reason their party will undoubtedly include a note-taker whose detailed minutes will be so fully circulated afterwards, including to people not present at the meeting, that they might come back to embarrass you, aeons later, when quoted by someone present or not at the meeting.

2. They are not averse, when **negotiating**, to trying to trip you up and/ or embarrass you and/or go over old ground with you, to which the most effective riposte is comprehensive notes.

3. Also, they are prone to asking interminable and multiple questions all in a single long sentence – which you will find much easier to answer if it is transcribed and broken down into its component parts by your note-taker.

4. Similarly, you will also find it easier (as suggested below) to summarise any agreements reached:
   - at the end of the meeting, verbally
   - afterwards, in writing.

5. Finally: you need someone in your party who can monitor the performance of the interpreter – otherwise you may never know whether what you said and heard was really what your Chinese counterpart heard and said.

From the foregoing, it follows that there is no such thing in China as **speaking off the record**, since 'anything you say may be taken down and later used in evidence against you' by the Chinese when and however it benefits them.

Interpreters

It is common practice for the Chinese to conduct meetings with foreigners via interpreters – even those who speak foreign languages do so, as a **ploy** to gain face-saving thinking time and/or **status symbol** to enhance their importance.

Do not be surprised, therefore, if your Chinese interlocutors address you in perfect English at the end of the meeting: they may well have studied for a post-graduate degree at a Western university.

For the same reason, never make *sotto voce* comments in your own language, in case you are overheard and understood.

Whatever the occasion or type of encounter in China, I (as a linguist) suggest the following guidelines:

1. Provide your own interpreter, even if you speak Chinese: or else your Chinese counterparts may wrongly conclude that you are not:
   - senior enough to warrant one
   - their equal
   which would cause them a loss of 'face', for the reason explained above.

2. Always talk to, and maintain eye contact with, your interlocutor – never the interpreter:
   - not only out of respect

– but also because it is the tone, inflection and pace of your voice etc. that is important – not the interpreter's.

3. Ensure that your interpreter understands the:
   – overall key aims and objectives of the meeting, as mentioned above
   – importance of a successful outcome – when the interpreter too may bask in the reflected glory and thereby gain 'face' by proxy.

4. Ensure that you have someone else in your party, apart from the interpreter, who is bilingual (such as the note-taker) in order to ensure that the interpreter:
   – fully and clearly conveys your message in an appropriate tone
   – does not start to converse directly with your interlocutor
   and:
   – agree how they will interact without either losing 'face' (e.g. if the interpreter makes a mistake or is stuck for a word).

5. Help your interpreter by:
   – advancing a transcript or summary of what you intend to say; and key vocabulary
   – talking at a steady pace, dividing your delivery into manageable whole sentences
   – using clear, jargon-free and unambiguous language
   – avoiding idioms, inappropriate humour, jokes and off-the-cuff remarks which may embarrass the Chinese if inaccurately translated.

6. Be aware that interpreters often enjoy intimate relationships with their principals and/or wield influence in their own right.

EXAMPLE

The interpreter for the then Vice-Mayor of Shanghai at a meeting which I attended in China turned up in London a year later running a training establishment for Chinese managers and offered me a paid speaking engagement.

Thus, the female interpreter of a Chinese man may also be his mistress for which reason, ensure your relationship with your interpreter (or Chinese bilingual PA, as in my case) is seen to be above reproach.

PRELIMINARIES

Whatever the occasion, the protocol regarding the **arrival, welcome** and **introductions, name cards** (i.e. business or visiting cards) and **seating** are similar, if not the same.

Arrival

For the Chinese, **punctuality** is a virtue, and tardiness an insult. Thus:

◆ **visitors** should arrive on time – neither late nor early

◆ **hosts** should assemble earlier in the meeting room ready to greet the visitors – to keep people waiting is even ruder

◆ **latecomers** should apologise profusely – in order to show that they meant no insult.

EXAMPLE
To ensure that my international board members arrived 'just in time' for meetings with senior Chinese government officials, my driver used to estimate journey times by making practice runs in the Beijing rush-hour.

On arrival, **visitors** should be: **met** by the hosts' representative (for example at reception); and **accompanied** to the meeting room – which, following Chinese custom, the visitors should enter in the hierarchical order of the:

1. most senior visitor
2. interpreter
3. other visitors in rank order.

This practice allows the Chinese easily to identify the **principal visitor** and main secondary visitors; otherwise, they may mistake whomever does enter first as the principal visitor.

If the Chinese greet the foreigners with **applause**, the correct response is to applaud (not wave) back.

Welcome and introductions

The principal host and visitor should introduce members of their party in same way as in the West, in **rank order**.

However, in accordance with Chinese business hierarchy:

♦ Where participants are of equal level, or in informal situations, introductions should be in **age order** (starting with the eldest), in deference to the Chinese respect for their elders.

♦ **Women** should be introduced to men – e.g.: 'Miss Xu, I would like you to meet Mr Smith'.

Senior Chinese officials seldom hold meetings with foreigners alone: staff members are invariably present. Do not be surprised, therefore, if the Chinese participants out-number your party, since superiority of numbers is just one method that the Chinese use to try to put foreigners in their place.

Not only for this reason will some Chinese participants not necessarily be introduced: those who are not are usually observers or apprentices, with no active role to play or sometimes covert Party members.

Unusually, refreshments may accompany the welcome occasionally, even delaying proceedings.

EXAMPLE

On first meeting a college principal, prior to a prize-giving, I was offered fruit – to have refused which would have been rude, even though it meant keeping the students waiting.

During introductions:

♦ Greet the Chinese appropriately, following the guidelines for forms of address.

♦ Smile (remembering that they may not respond).

♦ Bow slightly (by nodding your head, not bending at the waist) and exchange business, visiting or **name cards**, as explained below.

Name cards

In China, visiting or business cards are usually called **name cards** (*ming pian*); and their exchange and scrupulous study form an important part of meeting and greeting all and sundry.

Having name cards means you are 'somebody'; conversely, not having name cards may be interpreted as your not being very important.

Similarly, the more name cards the Chinese receive, the more (foreign) people they have met and important they feel or are perceived thus increasing their 'face' and *guanxi*.

EXAMPLE

One of my Chinese colleagues took pride in showing off her albums of name cards.

Thus, just having name cards is the first step to doing business successfully with the Chinese. Collecting them also serves: as a simple means of building up a contact database; and to show to taxi drivers on subsequent visits to China.

It is important, therefore, always to: have an ample supply of name cards (at least a boxful at any one time) in your briefcase; and carry enough for the day's meeetings on your person – preferably in a silver or leather card-holder, to create a good impression.

One word of caution: ensure you do not hand on someone else's card that you have just received.

EXAMPLE

I carried a leather card-holder with one pocket for cards 'in' and another for cards 'out'.

Name cards should:

♦ be **printed** on both sides: one in English; the other in Chinese, using simplified characters

♦ **include** your: company name, logo and business nature; name and meaningful job title; permanent contact details (postal and e-mail address; and phone and fax numbers); and, if a visitor, local contact details (e.g. mobile phone number).

EXAMPLE

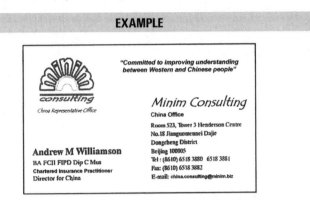

Author's name card — ↑ English and ↓ Chinese side

The more post-nominal letters the better – especially post-graduate or equivalent, which particularly impress the Chinese (since your most senior counterparts will be similarly qualified).

EXAMPLE

My most senior female Chinese colleague was not only very proud of her two post-graduate qualifications, but also claimed that was why she empathised with my wife, who is similarly qualified!

If you have difficulty having bilingual cards printed in your home country, most Western-style hotels are able to produce them very quickly.

On a practical note: have a copy of your company logo to hand; and arrange with a Chinese-speaking colleague to check both language versions to ensure they make sense and are compatible.

Seating

Important visitors are escorted to their seats, with the principal visitor being placed in the seat of honour to the right of the principal host (or facing, if at a table). Others may sit where they like – though it is customary to sit in descending rank order.

EXAMPLES

Interpreter		Interpreter
Visitor No.1		Host No.1
Visitor No. 2		Host No.2
Participant		Participant
Note-taker		Note-taker

Door

Simple meeting seating plan ⇧ without ⇩ with central table

Participant or Note-taker		Participant or Note-taker
Interpreter		Host No. 2
Visitor No. 1	Table	Host No.1
Visitor No. 2		Interpreter
Participant or Note-taker		Participant or Note-taker

Door

THE STRUCTURE OF MEETINGS

Meetings between foreigners and Chinese officials are not free exchanges but structured dialogues between the principals on both sides. Other participants act as witnesses, and speak only on their principal's explicit invitation. To interrupt a speaker is rude.

EXAMPLE

When accompanying my international board members on visits to senior Chinese government officials, I occasionally had to bite my tongue when they inadvertently deviated from the agreed speech, and wait until invited to speak to supply the missing or correct information without causing anyone any loss of 'face'.

Opening gambit

Chinese meetings begin with small talk. To dive right into the matter in hand is an impolite breach of etiquette. Avoid the temptation of laying all your cards on the table at the outset; rather, start with ice-breakers like general observations or questions before easing into the focus of the meeting, as follows:

1. **Thank** the principal Chinese host for taking time out from their 'undoubtedly' busy schedule.

2. **Remind** them fondly of the last meeting(s) they and/or their colleagues had, and the positive outcome for both parties.

3. Convey **greetings** from senior colleagues present at that meeting, but not at this.

4. **Compliment** them on the progress that the host department/ company/ministry etc has made since that last meeting, not forgetting to speak favourably of the advancement of China in general.

5. **Congratulate** them on any personal achievements (e.g. promotion).

6. **Outline** the purpose of the meeting.

7. **Mention** who the senior colleagues present are, particularly if the

principal host and/or his senior colleagues have met them before.

Whilst this may seem sycophantic, it should reflect the protocol that the principal Chinese host will follow.

The **Chinese principal** will not interrupt; and may reply in similar vein, including a lecture on China for the 'illiterate' foreigners. However boring or familiar, remember that someone has taken the trouble to prepare a brief in an attempt to be helpful. Smile, and show appreciation by later asking clarifying questions (to prove that you were listening and pretend that it was for the first time).

Exchange

In the exchange that follows, the Chinese will normally invite the **foreign principal** to speak first. This is not just good manners, but – given their aforementioned preference for reacting to others' ideas, rather than setting the agenda themselves – a ploy for the Chinese to gain the upper-hand by safely lobbing the ball back into the foreigner's court and back-footing him.

The exchange between the two principals may take two forms:

1. A lengthy and exhaustive discourse by the first speaker, followed by an equally lengthy reply (like a **debate**).

2. An exposition of, and immediate reply to, several individual points (like a **ping-pong** match).

Whilst both forms are acceptable, you should declare at the outset which one you propose to use.

EXAMPLE

I was once invited to explain to representatives of the PBOC and People's Insurance Company of China (PICC) the range of insurance competence and training schemes and professional qualifications in the UK – a complex and, to the uninitiated, possibly confusing subject.

After some 20 minutes of uninterrupted (and prepared) speaking, I paused for questions only to be asked to carry on!

Whichever form the exchange takes, you will need a good memory! Because Chinese education still encourages learning by rote, when you:

◆ **speak**: the less reference to notes and the greater the eye contact you can make, the more favourable the impression you are likely to cause

◆ **reply**: the Chinese will expect you to emulate them by remembering and dealing with all the points in the order raised.

When in doubt, opt for the second ('ping-pong') form of exchange, which is kinder on the attention span of all concerned.

One word of warning: if your Chinese counterpart nods or grunts whilst you are speaking, he is merely indicating his understanding *not* agreement.

Photographs
Do not be surprised if a Chinese participant takes photos of the meeting, to add to their collection of *guanxi* memorabilia for the same reasons as name cards, mentioned above.

TECHNIQUES
In addition to the normal guidelines for negotiating with the Chinese:

Sell – not tell
When putting forward your ideas:

Do...
◆ **ask** the Chinese what:
  – they need
  – you could do that would help them

◆ **suggest** your offering as their solution.

Do not...
◆ **remind** the Chinese what you have done for them in the past

◆ **tell** them what you:
  – are going to do for
  – want from

them in the future – which not only reveals your hand but also demonstrates a total disregard for their needs and 'face'

◆ **tell** them:
– what they need
– that you have the solution.

In other words: **make your solution their idea.**

Asking and handling questions

When asking and handling questions:

Do...

◆ wait until the speaker has finished before asking questions

◆ ask **clarifying questions** only

◆ say that you will get back with the reply to a **difficult question** which you cannot immediately answer

◆ defer with a face-saving reason when caught off guard (the Chinese will!).

Do not...

◆ put anyone 'on the spot' by asking an **unrelated question**, which could result in loss of 'face' for the Chinese if they do not know the answer

◆ introduce a **new request**, since the Chinese do not make off the cuff decisions, as mentioned above

◆ put colleagues on the spot

◆ say 'no' or 'I don't know'.

EXAMPLE

After listening to several lengthy simultaneously-translated speeches in Chinese at the Centenary Roadshow in Beijing of the CII, I (who was sitting on the podium), was asked by the Chairperson, without any warning, to respond to the Chinese speakers. That was one favour I was later able to call in!

Asking favours and making promises

Following the rules for 'face' and reciprocity, I recommend the following guidelines for asking favours and making promises:

Do...

♦ offer a way out, to save the 'face' of the Chinese

♦ remember the rules of reciprocity.

Do not...

♦ put the Chinese principals on the spot by asking them for:
  − something they cannot deliver
  − a promise they cannot keep which would be a loss of 'face'

♦ make rash promises that you cannot keep or have no intention of keeping.

Otherwise, in the wake of an impossible request, the tone of the meeting will slowly but surely cool.

EXAMPLE

I know of one foreigner who − carried away by the hitherto bonhomie of the moment − threw caution to the wind and asked the Chinese principal: when would his company be granted such-and-such favourable trading terms? The atmosphere subtly became less friendly, since the terms were not in the gift of the Chinese principal, who was noticeably embarrassed.

CLOSING AND FOLLOWING UP A MEETING

The meeting may come to a natural close; or when the principal host decides (e.g. by summing up; or making some suitable face-saving excuse, such as the visitors' tiredness) at which time I recommend the following guidelines for closing a meeting:

Do...

♦ **summarise** what was achieved or agreed (including action points) at the meeting to avoid any misunderstanding

♦ agree a **contact name** on both sides for future dealings.

Do not...
◆ forget to hand over your **gifts**.

Before formally taking leave, the Chinese may suggest a formal group photograph, even if an informal one was taken during the meeting.

To take your leave:
◆ shake hands and smile
◆ say *zai jian!* ('goodbye', literally 'again see')
◆ bow slightly (by nodding your head, not bending at the waist).

Thereafter, it is common practice for:

◆ The **Chinese principal** to exit the meeting room immediately, as a sign that the formalities are over and it is time to relax.

◆ A **member of the host party** (e.g. the interpreter) to accompany the visitors to the exit – contrary to Western practice: having brought the meeting to an abrupt ending, the Chinese tend to protract the farewells.

Follow up

As soon as possible after the meeting, I recommend the following guidelines for following up a meeting:

Do...

◆ send a '**thank-you letter**' to the Chinese, in their own language, **summarising** what was achieved or agreed at the meeting (including action points) to avoid any misunderstanding

◆ '**review to improve**' for next time.

HELPFUL HINT

The worst gaffe I committed was on meeting unexpectedly the then Governor of the PBOC at a college prize-giving at which we both were VIP guests – when the conversation ran as follows:

> Governor: Such-and-such a statesman was speaking to me last week about your company.

> Author (feigning surprise): What did he say?

Governor (with a straight face): What you told him to!

From this example stems a final word of advice. Make it clear to your Chinese colleagues that:

◆ **you** are the expert on your company's business

◆ **they** are the experts on China and doing business with the Chinese.

EXAMPLE
I was wont to ask my Chinese advisers to treat me like a **glove puppet**, and tell me what to say.

APPLICATION
The following protocols are specifically referred to again in subsequent chapters, as follows.

Topic	See Chapter
Business Meetings	5, 7, 8
Interpreters	8, 10
Note taking	5, 7

7

Business Entertaining

This chapter details the protocol for business entertaining in general, and **banquets** in particular, between the Chinese and foreigners – the correct observance of which should help build *guanxi*.

UNDERPINNING INFLUENCES, BEHAVIOURS AND PROTOCOLS FOR BUSINESS ENTERTAINING

Whilst the degree of formality may vary – according to the nature and importance of the occasion, and the number of and the relationship between the people involved – the underpinning influences, behaviours and protocols are the same.

Influence, behaviour or protocol	See chapters
Attitude to foreign women	2
Business meetings	6
Connections (*guanxi*)	3
Dress and jewellery	6
Exchanging gifts and favours	4
Face (*mianzi*)	3
General behaviour	3
Golden rule of Confucianism: reciprocity (*shu*)	1 and 4
Key concepts of Confucianism: generosity (*ren*)	1 and 4
Modesty and humility (*keqi*)	3
Negotiating techniques	5
Sexual equality at work	2
Sexually provocative clothing	3
Taboo subjects	3

Generosity takes many forms: one of the most obvious and tangible of which is entertaining.

Business is no exception: hence, an integral part of the Chinese business scene (at home and abroad) is entertaining, which normally takes the form of a banquet that gives the host an opportunity to exercise generosity and demonstrate prosperity by offering a wide range of dishes served successively – to the extent of purposely over-ordering.

The common purpose is to build *guanxi*, for which reason constantly hosting and attending banquets is a regular feature of doing business with the Chinese.

MAKING ARRANGEMENTS

Whatever the occasion, the **how**, **when** and **with whom** to make arrangements for a banquet are similar to those for business meetings.

Invitations

For very formal banquets, printed invitations may be issued in English and/or Chinese (one or two weeks in advance) which recipients should answer – in writing or by telephone – and may need to produce to gain entry.

As elsewhere, the invitation should specify the host, date, time, venue and, where appropriate, the occasion and principal guest.

My numbered invitation to a banquet in honour of the British Premier – in English. Chinese side, see overleaf.

值英国首相托尼•布莱尔访华之际
中国英国商会及英国驻华大使馆
诚邀

Mr Andrew Williamson 先生/女士

参加一九九八年十月七日星期三晚上六点正
在凯宾斯基饭店大宴会厅举办的欢迎晚会。

Ticket No./票号 **581**

To ensure that they reach the right people on time, banquet invitations should be delivered personally (e.g. using your driver) or electronically (e.g. by fax and/or e-mail).

PREPARING FOR BANQUETS

Whatever the occasion, preparation for banquets should include **agenda setting** and **briefing** in similar fashion as for business meetings – since either party may take advantage of the conviviality to try to catch the other 'off guard' and negotiate new concessions or information.

Menu

Assuming that the banquet is held in a restaurant or similar, as suggested below, brave is the foreign host who chooses the menu for Chinese guests! It is safer to:

♦ Delegate this task to a Chinese colleague, adviser or *maître d'hôtel* who understands the peculiarities of the Chinese palate and stomach.

♦ Brief that person on how to select the menu from the following:

Options for choosing a banquet menu		
Dishes	**Option**	**Price per head**
standard *(like a Chinese restaurant in your home country)*	1.	fixed
special	2.	
	3.	unlimited

As a general rule, except on very informal occasions, I suggest the following:

Reasons for providing printed bilingual menus	
For whom	**Purpose**
Chinese	add to their collection of *guanxi* memorabilia – for the same reasons as name cards and photographs at business meetings
foreigners	know what they are eating (if they cannot read Chinese)!

Apart from the various dishes, the menu should detail the occasion, in the same way as the invitation mentioned above.

Most restaurants or similar are able to handle the production of menus, especially if you choose one of their standard banquet menus.

On a practical note: check your own language version to ensure it makes sense and that the food is acceptable to foreigners.

EXAMPLE

I once agreed to what I had heard as 'shrunken prawns' but which turned out to be 'drunken prawns' – i.e. alive, and supposedly (but not always) comatose!

Dress and jewellery

As a general rule, standard banquet attire is: a dark lounge suit and tie for gentlemen; and a demure dress or trouser suit for ladies.

There is no need to dress in formal evening wear, unless the invitation specifically so requests.

Jewellery should be tasteful and unostentatious.

LOGISTICS

When banqueting with the Chinese, apart from the general considerations in China of: **when** (i.e. timing), **where** (i.e. venue), **spouses** and **drivers**, non-Chinese should pay special attention to the peculiar issues, in China or elsewhere, of: **note-taking** and **interpreting**.

Timing

The timing of banquets should fit in with normal office hours, mentioned in Chapter 6 – not least because many smaller, private banquets may naturally follow on from a meeting.

Thus, as a general rule, I recommend the following:

Suggested banquet timetable				
Time	Meal	Duration	Start	Finish
mid-day	lunch	1 ½ hours	mid-day	2 p.m.
evening	dinner	2 hours	6 p.m.	8 p.m.

When organising an **evening banquet**, you should bear in mind that the Chinese prefer to start straight after and go from work; and finish at a reasonable hour, when they can still find public transport.

In my experience, the later start and finish times in the summer suggested by some writers (e.g. 7 p.m. and 9 p.m. respectively) are not convenient to the Chinese. Hence, should you try to start later than 6 p.m., you may discover that the Chinese diners cannot attend and/or get transport home.

Venue

Banquets are usually held in reserved private rooms in restaurants, hotels or clubs.

Round tables are preferred, as they seat more diners (ten to 12 each) and allow them to face each other.

Spouses

Despite China's sexual equality at work, Chinese spouses do not usually attend business banquets, even if the foreigners' spouses are invited.

As a general rule, when spouses are present at a banquet: they should be seated at the same table as their partners, where feasible; with the most honoured place for the principal guest's spouse being on the left-hand of the principal host.

Drivers

Ensure that arrangements are made to feed your guests' drivers, according to local custom (from providing a simple meal in a separate room, to giving them cash to buy their own food somewhere else).

Note-taking

Ensure that your group includes a bilingual note-taker (with the permission of the principal Chinese participant), for the same reasons as for business meetings – namely (in summary):

1. Someone in the Chinese party will undoubtedly make notes.

2. The Chinese often ask complicated questions which you will find easier to answer if written down.

3. You need to be able check the performance of whomever is interpreting.

Similarly: remember not to say anything off the record, however convivially tempting the occasion – it may be noted down and used by the Chinese later.

Interpreters

In addition to the considerations and guidelines for business meetings, you should agree beforehand how and when the interpreter(s) will eat.

EXAMPLE

At the first formal banquet which I attended in honour of a Vice-Minister of MOFTEC, the foreign guests were embarrassed that the Chinese interpreter was not expected to eat until the end of the meal.

PRELIMINARIES

Whatever the occasion, the protocol regarding the **arrival**, **welcome** and **introductions**, **name cards** (i.e. business or visiting cards) are similar to those for business meetings.

Arrival

In addition to the guidelines for business meetings:

Before eating, the (principal) hosts may invite the (principal) guests to: sit in easy-chairs; partake of tea and cigarettes; and briefly indulge in small-talk until the banqueting staff signals that all is ready.

Occasionally, you may be asked to sign a guest book or scroll – when, unless you are particularly adept at calligraphy in general, and drawing Chinese characters in particular, both with a brush, I recommend contenting yourself with writing an oversize signature with a felt-tip pen.

Seating

For all banquets, even the less formal ones, the organiser should work out beforehand where the principal host(s) and guest(s) will sit, according to the following guidelines:

1. Seating is **hierarchical**, based on rank. Thus:

- ◆ hosts should request or be sent beforehand a list of the guests' names, in rank-order, in order to prepare seating plans

- ◆ guests should wait to be shown to their seats, normally indicated by bilingual name cards (and/or, at large banquets, on table-plans displayed outside the banquet room and/or included with the ticket)

EXAMPLE

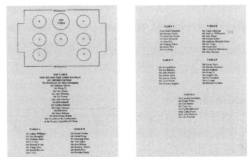

Seating plan included with my ticket for the banquet in honour of the then Deputy Secretary General of the State Council held at Lancaster House, London, April 1997.

2. As in the West, the **right-hand side** is of higher status than the left. Hence:

At a single-table banquet	
who	**should sit where**
guest No 1	on the right-hand of host No 1, and face the door
host No 1	on the left-hand of guest No 1, who faces the door
guest No 2	directly opposite guest No 1
host No 2	directly opposite host No 1
interpreters	on the right-hand side of guests Nos 1 and 2 (or opposite, at a square table) a practice that avoids them constantly having to swivel their heads

Example of a simple seating plan for a one-table banquet.

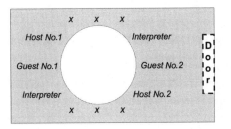

Alternatively:

At a multi-table banquet		
who	**should sit where**	
guests and hosts Nos 3 and 4	*either*	opposite each other at table No 2
	or	at the head of tables Nos 3 and 4, respectively
guests and hosts Nos 5 and 6 etc.	*either*	opposite each other at table No 3 etc.
	or	at the head of tables Nos 5 and 6, respectively etc.
top table	the furthest away from door	
other tables	so that each senior host can see and be seen by host No 1 at the top table	

3. With **mixed guests** (i.e. from different organisations), the most senior member of each delegation should sit at the top table.

So much for the theory!

In practice, one of two things may happen:

♦ At best: the list of Chinese guests may not be finalised until the last minute, since their acceptances or refusals could be telephoned very late for the same reasons as for business meetings.

♦ At worst: a guest who is unable to attend may send a substitute, possibly of different rank, which will upset the seating protocol.

GUIDELINES FOR BANQUET ETIQUETTE

Based on the rules of good behaviour described in earlier chapters, I suggest the following guidelines for banquet etiquette:

Toasting

Alcohol plays an important part in banquets, and should flow freely – when toasting is mandatory.

The main toasting drink is *maotai*, a 100% + spirit made in Maotai (Guizhou Province) from wheat and sorghum (a type of millet), which could be mistaken for lighter-fuel. You have been warned!

When toasting, you should observe the following guidelines:

1. Drinking alcohol should not start until after the **principal host** stands to propose the **first toast** with a speech (averaging three to five minutes) and/or the words *gan bei* (equivalent to 'bottoms up'; literally 'empty' or 'dry the glass').

2. A few courses later, it is customary and courteous for the **principal guest** to reply in similar fashion.

3. If **several tables** are used, it is customary and courteous for the **principal host and guest** to visit and propose a standing toast to each table, clinking glasses (rim to stem) with other principal guests.

4. Thereafter, anyone may propose a toast, to the group or individually, standing or sitting, spoken or silently, with alcohol or a soft drink.

5. Indeed, never drink alcohol alone, instead, catch someone's eye, make a silent toast by smiling, and drink together.

When proposing and replying to a toast, you should observe the following guidelines:

1. Hold the glass in both hands and extend it towards the toastee, without clinking, before drinking.

2. A token sip is quite sufficient and acceptable. (Hitherto, glasses were drained at one go and turned upside down. However, tradition has now been overtaken and replaced by the 'face' of sobriety, as explained below.)

3. At less formal banquets, Chinese now touch the table ('lazy Susan') with the bottom of their glasses, instead of clinking them.

Drinking

To observe the 'face' of sobriety, you should observe the following guidelines:

Do...

♦ **sip beer, soft drinks or tea** between toasts

♦ take care to **fill your neighbours' glasses,** when you should find that they will reciprocate

♦ **fill others' glasses as fully as possible,** without their spilling over, as a sign of respect and friendship

♦ be aware of the host who tries to make you drunk or challenge you to drinking games: it may be a matter of courtesy or honour for him to do so!

♦ **refuse alcohol politely** by:
   – turning your glass upside down or placing your hand over it
   – citing health reasons, if all else fails (e.g. allergy!)

♦ **continue to toast eagerly with a soft drink,** to save 'face'!

Do not...

♦ **fill your own glass** or cup if it is empty, which is impolite (by putting your needs above others')

♦ **stop drinking alcohol**, or change from hard to soft drinks, in the middle of a banquet, since the hosts may incorrectly conclude they have offended you

♦ **become drunk** or exhibit signs of drunkenness in public (e.g. staggering, falling, vomiting) which is unacceptable behaviour and a loss of 'face'

♦ **serve alcohol beforehand**, when you are the host.

Finally: although well-bred Chinese women do not drink alcohol (except beer) in public, **foreign female guests** may do so in moderation without incurring any shame, as the Chinese do expect foreigners to behave strangely!

Serving

When it comes to serving food, Chinese practice differs from Western, as per the following guidelines:

Where	What happens	
West	diners are served individual plates of food by waiters	or diners serve themselves
China	dishes are placed in the centre of the table for everyone – not only to share – but also to admire	and diners serve each other, not themselves

Appreciation of the presentation is almost as important as of the taste. Thus, **guests** are expected ritually to praise both – from time to time during, and at the end of, the banquet. Beware, however, of **ritually praising** food that you do not like: your host may remember, and serve the same again next time!

Equally, following the Chinese practice of ritual humility, the **host** should reply by **ritually apologising** for serving a meagre meal – which the cynics might consider false modesty fishing for compliments.

In the **absence of waiters**, it is the hosts' responsibility to monitor guests' plates and serve them throughout the meal – when, according to the rules of good behaviour described in earlier chapters, guests should observe the following guidelines for serving themselves:

Do...
- ◆ **after the first course** wait until the principal guests have been served before serving yourself

- ◆ serve yourself with
  - either **your chopsticks**
  - or the public chopsticks or serving spoons (if provided)

- ◆ help yourself to the **nearest dishes** and portions

- ◆ offer the choicest morsels to your **neighbours**, when you should find that they will reciprocate

- ◆ **serve others**, as a sign of respect and friendship

- ◆ when serving others: **if public chopsticks and serving spoons are out of reach**, reverse your chopsticks and use the end that has not been in your mouth.

Do not...
- ◆ start the **first course** until the principal host has:
  - either served the principal guest and others within chopstick reach (by selecting the best morsels and placing them on their plates)
  - or raised his chopsticks and invited the diners to eat

- ◆ **reach** across the table

- ◆ help yourself to the **best portions**

- ◆ serve others with a spoon used for personal eating.

Although Chinese protocol is to serve others rather than oneself, this practice is changing through foreign influence. You should, therefore: **observe how the Chinese diners behave and follow suit**.

Eating

As a general rule: to refrain from eating something is acceptable (albeit ungracious).

The main **exception** to this rule, however, is when your host serves you personally, even from his own plate, when he has probably chosen the most succulent morsel. On such an occasion, to refuse would be an insult: sometimes, you just have to grin and swallow (as I often had to).

Otherwise, **guests** can eat as much or little as they like of each course, according to their taste, without upsetting the host – when, in order not to cause offence, they should observe the following guidelines:

Do...
- **pace** yourself, eating slowly and steadily

- **sample** every dish – even if you only
  - lick the food
  - pop the food into your mouth and take it out again and put it back on your plate

- when faced with **something you dislike** or distrust:
  - accept but do not eat it
  - push it around on your plate a bit
  - pretend you have sampled it

- use your chopsticks or spit discreetly into a cloth **to remove something from your mouth**

- remember to **praise** the food, from time to time during, and at the end of, the banquet, as mentioned above.

Do not...
- **rush** or fill up too early

- **stop eating** in the middle of a banquet, which may lead the hosts incorrectly to conclude that they have caused you offence

- **refuse** food – which is:
  - at worst impolite

– at best ineffective, susceptible to being interpreted by the Chinese in their own terms as ritual modesty, not to be taken literally

♦ **use your fingers** to remove something from your mouth – since touching food is impolite, as mentioned below

♦ **over-praise** food you do not like, for reasons explained above.

Touching food

Touching food is generally impolite. There are some **exceptions**, however, such as using your fingers to eat large steamed buns, meat on the bone (e.g. chicken feet), Peking duck or shellfish – although using chopsticks is quite feasible. When in doubt: **do what the Chinese diners do**.

Chopsticks (*kwaizi*)

The most plausible reason that I have discovered for why the Chinese eat their food with chopsticks (*kwaizi*) rather than a knife and fork is that, in accordance with the teaching of Confucius, the latter symbolise violence – being reminiscent of cold-steel weapons – whereas chopsticks reflect gentleness and benevolence, key concepts of Confucianism.

Foreigners who have difficulty using chopsticks may use the porcelain spoon provided at each place setting – but only after having a go – which will not offend the Chinese, since they cannot all use a knife and fork.

EXAMPLES

1. I had to coach a Chinese college lecturer, who won a scholarship to study for a Masters degree abroad, how to use a knife and fork.
2. A senior British government official, of ambassadorial rank, whom I briefed at Farnham Castle International Briefing and Conference Centre (UK) – whilst writing this book – recounts how once his Chinese hosts, overwhelmed by the geniality of the occasion, bravely suggested that they should eat with knives and forks, and the foreigners with chopsticks. Needless to say, the ensuing scene was quite hilarious!

The Chinese use chopsticks any way they like, even spearing food with them (despite what other books may say).

EXAMPLE

At a small single-table banquet I attended, the principal Chinese guest – a Vice Minister, no less – not only used his chopsticks to spear his spring rolls, but also encouraged fellow diners to follow suit!

In keeping with the rules of good behaviour described in earlier chapters, diners should observe the following guidelines for using chopsticks:

Do...

◆ use your **right hand** (to avoid clashing with your neighbour)

◆ keep your **left hand** on the table (to avoid any speculation as to what it is doing)

◆ **hold the chopsticks** as near the top as possible (i.e. away from tip), which is considered a sign of good breeding

◆ **when not in use**, lay them on the rest provided or the rim of your plate.

Do not...

◆ **play** with your chopsticks

◆ **point** them at anyone

◆ **lay them** directly on the table

◆ **leave them in your rice-bowl** while doing something else (which is an omen of death, being reminiscent of incense sticks in a bowl of ashes offered to the dead)

◆ pick up food dropped on the floor – since touching food is impolite, as mentioned above.

Conversation

Normal rules of conversational etiquette in China apply, as for: business meetings, negotiating techniques and taboo subjects.

Thus: you may have to wait to be invited to speak (if you are not one of the principals); and, when you do, never speak off the record at a banquet (in case your words may come back to haunt you) and be aware of taboo subjects.

EXAMPLE

At my first formal banquet on a single-table hosted by a Vice-Minister of MOFTEC, I had to remain silent for nearly one hour.

In particular, your neighbours may not speak your language: however, if you do not know Chinese, you should still try to communicate with them somehow (e.g. in another language). Not to do so is a social blunder.

EXAMPLE

When my English wife found herself next to the Director General of CPAA, they were soon conducting a very animated conversation in Spanish!

Finally, some say: wait until after the fish dish has arrived to discuss business.

Gifts

In addition to the same general considerations and guidelines as for exchanging gifts and favours, I suggest the following particular guidelines:

When	What should happen
before	1. Each side should let the other know of its gift, to avoid the embarrassment of one party coming empty-handed and being unable to reciprocate.
	2. **Personal gifts** may be left at the place settings.
during	3. The **principal** or **communal gifts** (i.e. between the principal guest and host) should be presented publicly and formally at an appropriate moment (e.g. when making or responding to the main toast).

TABLE MANNERS

As a general rule, I suggest the following guidelines:

Bones Leave any bones and shells on your plate, which the waiters will remove and replace with a clean one.

Finger bowls After an especially messy dish for which using fingers is acceptable, as mentioned above, finger bowls may be provided to clean your hands, which should be dried on the towels provided, as mentioned below.

Nose blowing Blowing your nose in public is considered impolite at the best of times; but at table is positively rude. If you really have to: excuse yourself, and 'perform' in private. However, many uneducated Chinese ignore this rule in the street and dispense with a handkerchief, blocking one nostril with their finger, and blowing out of the other.

Smoking Smoking between courses is not unusual. Although Chinese **women** tend not to smoke, and especially in public, foreign female guests may do so in moderation without incurring shame, as the Chinese expect foreigners to behave oddly!

Tooth picks As elsewhere, use:
– one hand to wield the toothpick
– the other to hide your mouth from onlookers.

Towels Towels are provided at the beginning and end of the banquet for the diners to wipe their hands and face: hot in winter, cold in summer.

DISHES

As a general rule, banquets:

Start with... an even number (four to ten) of **cold appetizers**, such as: meat, seafood, pickled vegetables, peanuts (which will test your skills with chopsticks! – since touching food is impolite, as mentioned above).
These dishes do not count as part of the meal proper,

but are intended to whet the diners' appetites and accompany the **first toast**.

Include... **six to twelve main courses** comprising: hot meat, fish (*yu*) (see below), poultry, seafood, vegetable dishes, staple food, such as: rice (*mifan*) (see below), noodles (see below) and dumplings (*jiaozi*) and soup (see below).

End with **fruit**, which the Chinese consider an appropriate finale to a good meal, since they do not generally eat **dessert** and are unaccustomed to **cheese**.

Below is an example of the menu for the banquet in honour of the British Premier (Beijing, October 1998).

菜单
Menu

锦绣拼盘
Barbecued Meat Combination

腰果七彩炒鸡丁
Sauteed Diced Chicken with Assorted Vegetables and Cashew Nuts

豆腐鹅片
Sliced Goose with Bean Curd

黑椒牛柳粒
Diced Beef Tenderloin in Black Pepper Sauce

红烧鱼翅羹
Braised Shark's Fin and Fish Maw in Soup

清蒸桂鱼
Steamed Mandarin Fish with Light Soya Sauce

上汤菜心
Young Vegetables in Superior Broth

糯米荷叶饭
Glutinous Rice in Lotus Leaves

北京水饺
Beijing Pork Dumpling

中秋莲茸月饼
Traditional Moon Cake with Lotus Bean Paste

合时水果拼盘
Seasonal Fresh Fruit Platter

茶或咖啡
Tea & Coffee

Individual dishes

As a general rule, I suggest the following guidelines:

Fish   When serving fish, the head should point towards and be offered to the principal guest.

Also, as intimated above, some say: wait until the fish has arrived to discuss business.

Noodles   Do not be surprised if the Chinese diners eat the noodles noisily, as a way of showing the host their enjoyment and appreciation.

However, **eating noisily** on other occasions (e.g. soup) is no longer as acceptable as it used to be.

Rice   Since a banquet is a demonstration of the host's prosperity, as explained above, rice – as a staple food – may not always be served. Thus, as a general rule at a banquet, when rice is not served you should **never ask** for it. If it is served you need **only pick** at it, as a way of demonstrating your satisfaction.

Note: This is in contrast to private meals, where, in deference to the importance of rice in Chinese history and culture, to leave rice is impolite: just as Western children are encouraged to 'finish their greens', so Chinese children are to eat their rice.

Surprisingly, the **correct way to eat rice** is to raise the bowl to your mouth with one hand, and 'shovel in' the rice with the chopsticks.

Soup   Soup (a thin broth to aid digestion) may be served before or after the main courses, depending on where in China; and dispensed by the host. The bowl may be held in one hand, and the soup sipped from the bowl or using a porcelain spoon.

CLOSING AND FOLLOWING UP A BANQUET

Contrary to Western practice, it is the **host**, not the guests, who takes the initiative in bringing the proceedings to a close.

Thus, the banquet ends after the last course, with little ceremony beyond the **host** thanking the guests for coming; asking if they have had enough to eat – to which the polite reply is 'yes', as explained below; and rising from the table.

Chinese manners call for a speedy conclusion: to linger is impolite. Thus, there is no *Tischgespräch* or over-coffee table-talk.

Ensure, therefore, that your **transport home** is waiting for you at the end of the banquet: to be left standing around alone will embarrass your host.

Take your leave in the same way as after business meetings.

The host may bid the guests farewell (with a handshake) at the door; or accompany them to their cars, remaining outside, waving, until all have left – before returning to the restaurant, alone, to settle the bill.

Karaoke
Despite the foregoing: do not be surprised if you are invited by a Chinese host whom you know well to take part in a post-prandial **karaoke** session.

Thankfully, ability is not a prerequisite! Rather, the main purpose is pure enjoyment, as well as an excuse for further drinking (which can be expensive for the host).

If – like me – therefore, you are not a fan of karaoke, do not worry: one song and your ordeal is over; and your individual and corporate 'face' saved.

Showing appreciation
It is not only polite but also *de rigueur* for **hosts** to over-order, and **guests** to leave something on their plates to signify their hunger has been satisfied – for which reason:

◆ If all the food were consumed, or bowls emptied, the **host** would be embarrassed, thinking he had left the guests hungry.

◆ Before leaving, the **guests** should not hesitate to tell their host they have eaten enough.

Reciprocating

As a general rule at a banquet, when it comes to paying: the **host** settles the bill; and the **guests** reciprocate with a return banquet.

Thus, in the spirit of the Chinese proverb, quoted earlier, that **courtesy demands reciprocity**, the Chinese will expect you to 'reward' their hospitality in China with a farewell banquet, shortly before you return home. Otherwise, they will feel mortally offended by your lack of appreciation and, likely as not, fail to cooperate in the future.

Note: 'Going Dutch' (i.e. splitting the bill) is unheard of in China except between very close friends, when money should only be exchanged in private to avoid the host losing 'face'.

Follow up

As soon as possible after the banquet, besides reciprocating, you should follow up in the same way as after business meetings.

POSTSCRIPT

Some final thoughts.

New faces

Be aware that at a banquet accompanying negotiations new faces may appear who previously have not been part of such negotiations. They could be the real decision-makers who are too senior to attend the routine meetings. This is your opportunity to impress them.

Photographs

Do not be surprised if a Chinese participant takes photographs of the banquet, to add to their collection of *guanxi* memorabilia – in the same way and for the same reasons as for name cards during business meetings.

Helpful Hints

Food in China bears no relation to that served in Western Chinese restaurants. Indeed, there is a saying: 'the Chinese eat anything that flies, except aeroplanes; anything with four legs, except tables; and anything in the sea, except submarines.'

Only days after my first encounter with 'drunken prawns', mentioned above, I was the guest of honour at a College lunch, where the Principal's favourite dish was served as a great treat: **drunken prawns**...except that the prawns were very much alive, noisily and visibly jumping around inside a clear Pyrex dish! Thankfully, my 'face' was saved when the senior members of the college faculty all grimaced with one accord and persuaded the Principal to have the prawns cooked!

Indeed, not even my fulsome briefing of a British government official, mentioned above, prepared the latter for the 'shock' (his word) of the range of dishes offered by a hospitable Chinese host anxious to please. Whilst the soups and vegetables were most appetising, some meat dishes were so unpalatable by Western standards – such as: fish heads, calves' hooves and bulls' genitalia – that just their memory made him feel nauseous on the way to his third banquet in a row!

Abstaining, as intimated above, is a loss of 'face' for host and guest alike and, hence, not an option. For which reason, and to avoid any nasty surprises, I suggest the following tips for coping with Chinese food:

1. Refrain from **live food**.

2. If you do not recognise what you are eating, ask what it is after, not before, trying the food: sometimes it is better not to know – snake and alligator are really quite tasty!

3. Familiarise yourself with such **euphemisms** as: 'field chicken' for 'bullfrog'; and 'sea cucumber' for 'sea slug'.

4. If your Chinese hosts, colleagues and friends insist on trying out new dishes on you, do as I did:
   – ask if you can choose a dish
   – choose the most outrageous dish you dare
   – eat it with relish
   after which, they may not trouble you again!

5. Chinese food is often laced with **monosodium glutamate** (*weijing*), which swells inside you and makes you feel full. If you react badly to it, try asking in Western-style restaurants for food without MSG (*qing gei wo mei you weijing*).

6. To avoid going hungry and/or line the stomach – at breakfast (when your Chinese hosts will not normally be present):
   – **stoke up** with Western food
   – **stock up** on fruit (e.g. bananas) to eat later when you get a private moment to yourself.

Otherwise: **if you do not have a strong stomach, ask for an alternative assignment!**

APPLICATION

All the foregoing protocols are specifically referred to again in subsequent Chapters, as follows:

Protocol	See chapter
Business entertaining	8

8

Handling the Media

This chapter:

◆ **Outlines** the protocol for handling the media in China – the incorrect observance of which may easily spell disaster, even if proper adherence might not necessarily have any beneficial impact.

◆ **Assumes** a basic knowledge and understanding of public relations (PR) in general, onto which such specific protocol may be grafted.

◆ **Concentrates**, therefore, purely on the aspects peculiar to China.

UNDERPINNING BEHAVIOURS AND PROTOCOLS FOR HANDLING THE MEDIA

Whilst the degree of formality may vary – according to the nature and importance of the occasion, and the number of and the relationship between the people involved – the underpinning behaviours and protocols are the same.

Behaviour or protocol	See chapter
Bribes	4
Business entertaining	7
Business meetings	6
Consensus	3
Connections (*guanxi*)	3
Exchanging gifts and favours	4
Interpreters	3
Modesty and humility (*keqi*)	6

The common purpose is the same as elsewhere, namely: **public relations**, rather than and as distinct from advertising – that is: to build and enhance market profile, presence and reputation.

After all: why should the Chinese do business with Western 'foreign devils' unless we can win them over?

To that end, we should clearly, appropriately and publicly communicate to the Chinese people via the press and media the same messages as we do privately to their leaders at meetings and banquets.

SOURCING PR EXPERTISE AND ACHIEVING MEDIA COVERAGE

As elsewhere, the first challenges in China are: how to source **PR expertise** and achieve **media coverage** – to which I offer the following suggestions:

Sourcing PR expertise

In deciding on where to turn for help with handling the media in China, there are basically two options, of which the benefits of one parallel the drawbacks of the other.

Sources of public relations expertise in China		
	External consultants	**Internal resources**
F o r	International PR firms may employ staff (e.g. Western China-hands and/or Western-educated Chinese) who: ◆ understand local and international practice ◆ can, therefore, coach you in how to handle the Chinese media ◆ have *guanxi* in media circles	Such resources, since they are internal to the business, should be: ◆ cost-effective ◆ very familiar with your business, products and services ◆ no security risk, as they are subject to in-house confidentiality regulations ◆ in tune with your aims and objectives
A g a i n s t	Such firms, since they are external to the business, may be: ◆ very expensive ◆ unfamiliar with your business, products and services ◆ a security risk, as they necessarily have to be privy to your plans and secrets before they become public knowledge ◆ out of synch with your aims and objectives	Such resources, since they are internal to the business, may: ◆ not understand international practice ◆ be unable, therefore, to coach you in the differences between handling the Chinese and your home media ◆ not have sufficient *guanxi* in media circles ◆ be hard to recruit and/or not wholly competent without extra training

Such options, however, are not mutually exclusive.

For example I successfully combined the two, implementing the following mixed recipe for growing in-house expertise:

1. **Retain** an in-China PR firm that employs staff who understand the Chinese media and international practice.

2. **Reward** the consultants on a per-event rather than retainer basis, to encourage them to be proactive and earn their fees.

3. **Recruit** an in-house resource with the relevant and appropriate background and future potential.

4. **Retrain** the in-house resource by being fully involved and thus coached on-the-job by the external consultants.

5. **Release** the external consultants.

The hardest stage is the third: recruiting a potential in-house PR resource who, apart from a relevant and appropriate background, possesses integrity and – a rare commodity amongst the consensus-minded Chinese – initiative.

EXAMPLES

From a long short-list and even greater number of applicants, I whittled the credible ones down to two young Chinese ladies – and:

1. Appointed (as my personal assistant) a bilingual editor of the *China Daily*, with press experience and useful *guanxi* in media circles.

2. Rejected an ex-PLA intelligence officer whose PR methods and skills – to put it delicately – evoked those of James Bond's female adversaries!

Achieving media coverage

The question in China seems to be not whether but how much air-time or column-inches the media will give you – to which the answer is probably in direct proportion to how much money you give them! Not by way of a bribe, of course; but as a legitimate reimbursement of their working costs.

(Obviously, you must have a purpose – that is: something worth saying and hearing.)

Thus, from experience, it seems that the more you are prepared to spend (e.g. on broadcast production costs, entertaining media personnel, and journalists' 'expenses'), the wider and – no less important – more favourable the coverage.

EXAMPLES

In 1998, when:

1. Beijing TV wished to produce a programme tracing the history of insurance, they approached me, asking me not only to write the script (in English and Chinese), stage the filming in my office, provide the props and 'star', without plugging my own company; but also to pay some RMB 10,000 (approximately £750 or US$1200) for the privilege!

2. Entertaining (to breakfast or lunch) select bands of journalists in first-class Western-style hotels – besides providing press-packs and modest gifts – I had to arrange for my guests to be reimbursed some RMB 100 (approximately £8 or US$12) towards their taxi-fares, costing probably no more than a third of that amount: otherwise, they might not have attended, let alone reported favourably!

3. Holding morning press conferences finishing at lunchtime but not followed by lunch, I had to reimburse the journalists some RMB 200 (approximately £15 or US$24) towards their 'expenses'.

A subtler, cheaper and practical – albeit less reliable – way of gaining the media's attention is to frequent high-profile events – such as trade fairs – attired so as to stand out from the crowd.

EXAMPLE

Whilst this may sound far-fetched, my bow-tie gained me an unexpected television interview at the 1997 Tianjin Financial Services Exhibition.

A further method, of course, is *guanxi* – yours and the journalists'.

EXAMPLE

After a press lunch, one journalist asked for a private interview with me –
which led to a second journalist from the same paper (*China Business*)
requesting a personal interview with my wife and myself.

Another method used by other foreigners, but not me, is sponsoring
syndicated broadcasts or articles on relevant business-related subjects –
such as insurance, as one US insurer did.

Finally, as elsewhere, Chinese journalists (press and broadcast) are not
averse to 'freebies' – so why not include them on your guest list to
suitable events such as signing ceremonies, seminars and receptions?

DEALING WITH THE PRESS

The **general protocol** for press interviews, conferences, breakfasts and
lunches is similar to those for business meetings and entertaining,
where appropriate (e.g. making arrangements, preparation, logistics,
preliminaries and closure).

Particular protocol

Peculiar to China – in my experience, at least – are the:

♦ artificial **button-holes** (often with red ribbons stating in Chinese
that the wearer is a 'host' or 'most honoured guest'), **flower
arrangements** and **flags** of China and your home country

EXAMPLE

Press conference in January 1998 at Beijing's China World Hotel to launch the China Index Fund.

♦ red cloth **banners** spanning the wall behind the top table announcing in Chinese and English the purpose of the event – along the lines of: 'XYZ company welcomes the Beijing press to the announcement of its such-and-such product or service'.

EXAMPLE

Banners from the launch of the Britain in China Campaign, Beijing, January 1998.

Two variations on a theme are:

♦ Collecting **journalists' name-cards** is a simple method of keeping a:
  – record of the publications represented
  – check on whether the people whom you invited and who attended were the same – so that you know which publications and/or journalists to target in the future.

♦ Do not assume that all journalists can read English, but provide the principal hosts with **bilingual name-badges** including a meaningful job-title.

Press releases and articles

Press releases – whether solicited or speculative – should be translated into Chinese by a trustworthy native speaker, and reviewed by another, before being submitted, to ensure that the translation is accurate and acceptable to you.

Press packs

On their arrival at interviews, conferences, lunches and breakfasts, I recommend having a pack available for each journalist containing the following:

- press release relevant to the occasion

- transcript of any speeches (in full or summary)

- answers to 'frequently asked questions'

- description of your company, including an overview of your association with, and business plans in, China

- names, titles, career résumés and photos of the principal participants

- local contact details

  All the above in English and Chinese

- most recent company brochure(s) and accounts

- modest gift

- reimbursement of taxi fares.

Paradoxically, in a country where freedom of expression is relatively limited, the more editorial control that you can exercise over what is reported in print, the closer the final article should be to what you originally intended

Journalists' club

One method of drip-feeding information to the press is to form an inner-circle or club of those journalists who can best serve your cause; and invite them regularly to private meetings and other 'closed' events.

Interpreters

In addition to the considerations and guidelines for business entertaining and meetings:

As a result of the normally intimate and closed nature of their work, and of the virtue that the Chinese place on modesty, some interpreters may be uncomfortable with the limelight into which a **press conference** necessarily throws them – for which reason, you should check that your interpreter has:

◆ The ability to **speak in public** and/or **freely interact with strangers**, skills required to deliver your speeches in Chinese and/or interpret any question-and-answer sessions. For example, as a qualified choir trainer, I coached my interpreter in voice projection.

◆ A suitable **wardrobe**, reflecting the image that you wish to project of your company. For example, I bought my interpreter (i.e. my Chinese bilingual PA) a smart suit for just such occasions.

Such interpreters are rare, having to be groomed – which is perhaps why mine was borrowed on several occasions, including by the then British Ambassador!

EXAMPLE

The very public and up front role of an otherwise modest interpreter (far left) at a press conference in Shanghai to celebrate the signing of a Memorandum of Understanding.

Master of ceremonies
Press conferences need a master of ceremonies – which is an ideal opportunity for your 'man on the ground' (rather than an external PR firm) to raise their personal profile (as I can vouch).

TELEVISION AND RADIO BROADCAST
Unless you speak Chinese, you may expect and be expected to talk in English or your own language and should employ your own interpreter.

Exceptionally and alternatively: for long **television** programmes, it may suffice to provide a translation of your words for the producer to arrange a voice-over. This was the case when I spoke at length on the history of insurance on Beijing TV.

In either event: even if you do not speak the language, do make the effort to rehearse and include one or two phrases in Chinese.

At the other end of the scale: do not forget to invite broadcast journalists to your press conferences.

HELPFUL HINTS
I am grateful to my Chinese ex-Personal Assistant (whose media credentials are mentioned above) for suggesting the following tips for handling the Chinese media:

1. Obtain **background information** on the media; and, if possible, read the press, listen to the radio and watch the television.

2. Try to find out what **questions** will be asked. Many Chinese reporters will not mind giving you a list of questions before interview, even if only a few of them may stick to the list! Nevertheless, this will give you an idea of the sort of questions they might ask, and their areas of interest. Even when they go beyond the list, Chinese reporters rarely ask aggressive questions: indeed, they are generally much less aggressive than their international counterparts.

3. Talk about your **investment in China**. If you are not currently investing in China, tell them about any future plans to do so. Such investment is not necessarily just in cash, but can include:

seconding foreign experts, staging public training events, offering scholarships, sponsoring visiting artists or opening a representative office – in other words: your **commitment to China**. This should increase the chance of what you say being published and receiving better coverage.

4. Quote **figures**: they love that.

5. Provide information about **Western practice** in your business – for example: the regulatory framework.

6. **Never criticise** the Chinese government or business regulatory regime. Rather, **praise** China, Chinese culture, the local market etc.

7. Present **gifts**, even if only modest.

8. Distribute corporate brochures, press releases (including previous ones), product flyers etc. – in short: any **written material** related to your business; and, if applicable, **product samples**.

APPLICATION

The following topic is specifically referred to again in a subsequent chapter, as follows.

Topic	See Chapter
Sourcing PR Expertise	10

9

Market Entry Strategies

This chapter:

◆ **Briefly suggests** various strategies for foreign businesses still thinking of or in the process of trying to enter the Chinese market.

◆ **Assumes** a basic knowledge and understanding of the underlying business principles – such as: government relations, marketing, sponsorship, strategic thinking, JVs, due diligence etc.

◆ **Concentrates**, therefore, purely on the aspects peculiar to China.

◆ Refers to the following underpinning influences and behaviours:

Influence or behaviour	See chapter
Business environment	1
Chinese politics	3
Connections (*guanxi*)	3

OVERVIEW OF STRATEGIES
The suggested strategies, detailed below include:

Political profiling
Be recognised by the Chinese and your governments and regulatory authorities as meeting the legal requirements for an operating licence, and having the technical competence to operate a business, in China.

Relationship management
Sign a joint venture agreement with an acceptable Chinese business partner.

Marketeering

Be ready to operate in any market likely to be open to foreign companies in the short to medium term and offering long-term profitable growth.

Human resource management

Have an occupationally competent local work force.

All four strategies are interdependent and should, therefore, progress in parallel, such that as the milestones of one are achieved so are those of the other three.

Disclaimer

Although such strategies are:

◆ **generic** – that is: not specific to any particular business or market sector – they are not all automatically suitable for each and every business and market

◆ based on **experience** – albeit vicarious – they do not necessarily guarantee success.

LONG-TERM COMMITMENT

Entry to China requires long-term commitment for a number of reasons – as follows.

There is a long queue of foreign companies hoping to do business in China, for which:

◆ an **operating licence** is needed

◆ a '**probationary period**' may also be required, for similar reasons as new employees by their Western employers.

The qualifications for the former and details of the latter will depend on the:

◆ **business** – such as: manufacturing, retail or financial services

◆ **operation** – such as: wholly owned foreign enterprise (WOFE), JV, branch or representative office

◆ **government-to-government relationships**.

The first insurance licences were granted at the rate of one country (per continent) per year – often depending on their relationship with China.

◆ **legal criteria** – which may be over-shadowed by such political considerations

all of which are outside the scope of this chapter and book.

Suffice it to say, therefore, that the various hoops through which you may have to jump could take considerable time – by your standards.

However, such waiting time need not necessarily be unproductive. Indeed, quite the opposite: it is an opportunity to:

◆ not only **demonstrate your worth** – such as: value to China

◆ but also **thwart the competition** by persuading the Chinese that you are more worthy than your competitors – for example: using some of the appropriate strategies mentioned below.

My brief was to direct the company's China Market Entry Team in order to be the natural choice for the next licence issued by the Chinese government in our business sector.

It is probably no exaggeration to say that such 'hoops' are designed to help the authorities:

◆ 'sort the wheat from the chaff', in general

◆ test your **patience**, in particular.

Whatever the four 'Ps' of marketing may stand for in the West, in China they all mean **patience**.

Occasionally in the past, some foreign companies have tired of waiting and retreated from China, hoping to return at a more opportune moment – for them, that is, but not necessarily the Chinese who may well consider such a retreat as typical of fickle and self-interested outsiders, and thus never allow them back.

For foreigners, there is no such thing as making a quick buck in China, since the necessary set-up:

♦ **time** – for example to build *guanxi*

♦ **costs** – such as involved in proving your worth and thwarting the competition, mentioned above

may – nay, will – take several years.

China is not for the impatient!

STRATEGIES

Political profiling

In view of the role of the Chinese Government in approving licence applications, mentioned above, I suggest the following (untried) three-year plan for politcal profiling:

During year 1 **position** to the Chinese and your governments and regulatory authorities your **business aspirations and credentials** in China – by:

1. preparing **business plans**

2. submitting a **licence application** to the Chinese regulatory authority (centrally and at individual market level)

3. officially notifying the Chinese and your governments and embassies; and subsequently indulging in **political lobbying**

4. undertaking appropriate **profile raising** activities that:
   a) enhance the **company's image**
   b) demonstrate **long-term commitment** to China
   c) achieve significant **on-going dialogue** with influential parties such as:
      – **sponsorship** (such as: cultural, and/or educational)
      – media and **public relations**
      – **senior level visits** from your head office
      – local **community action**
      – the Chinese and your Embassies and Chambers of Commerce.

During year 2 **develop and present** to the Chinese government and regulatory authorities your detailed **business start-up plan** – by:

1. drawing on **your company's expertise** in other territories

2. learning from your local **competitors' mistakes**

3. focusing on **distribution channels** and **operating methods** that match your business needs and satisfy any regulatory requirements

4. realigning the programme of **profile raising** activities to the evolving business environment.

During year 3 **demonstrate** to the Chinese government and regulatory authorities your **operational competence** – by:

1. drawing on your **company's experience and success stories** in other territories

2. successfully implementing your business start-up plan.

Relationship management

In the present context of market entry strategies, the purpose of *guanxi* may be redefined as:

♦ to identify, build and nurture a **circle of friends** whose influence and/or expertise can assist you to achieve your overall corporate objective of positioning your company with the relevant governmental and regulatory authorities as a suitable candidate for an operating licence in China

and translated into:

♦ influencing governmental advisers and decision-makers (as described above)

♦ gathering market intelligence

♦ building a future client base

♦ finding a JV partner.

The last is not that dissimilar to finding a life or marriage partner – on the basis of which model, I suggest the following (untried) three-year plan for securing a JV partner:

During year 1 **short-list** and hold informal negotiations with a small number of potentially suitable eligible JV partners – by:

1. cataloguing any existing circle of friends, including potential JV partners

2. defining the JV partner search-criteria, according to the legislation and business needs

3. short-listing potentially suitable and eligible JV partners according to their assessment against those criteria – akin to a **beauty contest**

4. courting the short-listed potential JV partners – akin to **two timing**.

During year 2 reach **provisional agreement** with a single potentially suitable, eligible and willing JV partner – by:

1. refining the JV partner search-criteria, according to the legislation and business needs

2. selecting one preferred potential JV partner, according to an in-depth assessment against the refined JV search criteria – akin to a **proposal of marriage**

3. being ready to sign a MOU with the selected JV partner.

During year 3 sign a **formal agreement** with the selected JV partner – by:

1. signing a MOU with the selected JV partner – akin to a **pre-nuptial agreement**

2. alternatively: receiving a proposal from a suitable and eligible JV partner – akin to **Leap Year's Day**.

Marketeering

In order to be fully operational at the earliest opportunity, I suggest the following (untried) three-year plan for marketeering:

During year 1 **identify potentially profitable markets** opening to foreign companies – by:

1. appraising the potential of the markets where competitors currently operate and are represented

2. carrying out appropriate research of other markets

3. consulting with reliable sources of political and economic information.

During year 2 **short-list and develop a suitable presence** in (say) five such markets – by:

1. establishing **representative offices** where these do not already exist

2. confirming the company's commitment to China by becoming one of the few 'large' representative organisations (with five or more representative offices)

3. undertaking **targeted profiling**

4. courting the local representatives of your company's circle of friends, especially of the short-listed potentially suitable and eligible JV partners

5. ensuring that activities in one market support and complement activities in other markets as part of a **pan-China strategy**

6. designing a generic operating infrastructure capable of rapid local transplantation – by:
   a) developing a blueprint for a central **model office**
   b) finding suitable **premises** acceptable to the local regulatory authorities
   c) identifying suitable **technology** and systems capable of local support
   d) identifying **distribution channels** independent of any potential or preferred JV partner.

During year 3 **establish a suitable local market operation** – by implementing the design for a generic operating infrastructure capable of rapid local transplantation.

Human resource management

The following chapter (10) is wholly devoted to human resource management.

(10)

Human Resource Management

This chapter examines the more important, but not all, HRM issues facing foreigners who manage or have management control over Chinese employees in a foreign-owned or foreign-invested company in China.

All the underpinning influences, protocols and behaviours have already been addressed in previous chapters and many illustrated with examples and/or case studies centred on those issues, as follows:

HR issue	Influence, behaviour or protocol	Chapter
Authority	Deferring to authority Exercising authority *Laobanism*	3
Decision making	Changing your mind Consensus Deferring to authority	3
Disciplining staff	Conflict management Disciplining staff	3
Drivers	*Laobanism*	3
Employment law	Legal environment	1
Equal opportunities	Sexual equality at work	2
Honesty and dishonesty	Harmony Making mistakes	3
Interpreters	Interpreters	6
Job titles	Losing and saving 'face'	3
Loyalty and disloyalty	Family and friends Whose 'face' is it anyway?	2 3

Mixed race staff	Attitude to foreigners Overseas Chinese	2
Personal assistants	Exercising authority	3
Praising staff	Giving 'face'	3
Private offices	Losing and saving 'face'	3
Problem solving	Practice of *guanxi*	3
Promotion	Dead men's shoes Eight Dos and Don'ts	3 1
Rank and hierarchy	Business hierarchy Filial piety	3 1
Recruitment	Building *guanxi* Eight Dos and Don'ts Practice of *guanxi* Sourcing PR expertise	3 1 3 8
Reprimanding staff	Conflict management Losing and saving 'face'	3
Rewarding staff	Iron rice bowl Staff gratuities	1 4
Staff relations	Business hierarchy 'Laobanism'	3
Status (symbols)	Exercising authority	3
Team working	'Face' by proxy Collectivism	3
Training	Education system Face Modesty and humility Sourcing PR expertise	2 3 3 8
Upward delegation	Deferring to authority	3

This chapter, therefore, complements and expands on those examples and/or case studies – the majority of which are drawn from Chapter 3, as indicated above, and mainly fall into the two categories of **'face'** and **hierarchism** – rather than repeat what has gone before

Hence I suggest that you review that chapter before reading this one.

Caveat

This chapter is illustrative rather than exhaustive, in that it:

♦ **Assumes** a basic knowledge and understanding of HRM best practice – for example: as espoused in the UK by Investors in People (IiP) or the Chartered Institute of Personnel and Development (CIPD) (of which I am a Fellow).

♦ **Concentrates**, therefore, purely on the aspects peculiar to China.

Moreover, it is included here rather than in any book about working *in* China, since it is quite possible and legitimate for some foreigners to do so without working very much or at all *with* the Chinese (e.g. in international or language schools).

Western HRM with Chinese characteristics

Implementing Western HRM practice lock, stock and barrel could be as disastrous as the wholesale acceptance of the Chinese status quo – if not more so, should your workforce resist the former (insofar as, and in whatever form, the Chinese are wont to resist).

Thus, rather than throwing out the baby with the bath water, I – as an ex-HRM professional:

♦ Contest the view of those commentators who maintain that China is hostile to Western HRM practice – otherwise: why do so many Chinese prize an overseas MBA degree?

♦ Recommend adapting the best of the former to take account of the underpinning protocols and behaviours of the latter to produce **Western HRM with Chinese characteristics** – as described below.

HUMAN RESOURCE MANAGEMENT STRATEGY

In order to achieve your market entry strategy, as discussed in Chapter 9, you will need a parallel HRM strategy – for which I suggest the following three-year plan for developing a local work-force:

During year 1, **establish a cost-effective and competent core workforce** – including by:

1. adopting a policy of localisation (as far as possible) – for example, by:
   a) filling as many jobs as possible with mainland Chinese staff on local terms
   b) standardising employment contracts

2. adopting a fair and competitive rewards system – for example, by introducing:
   a) performance management system
   b) simplified job and performance related salary scales

3. adopting competence-based selection, assessment and development schemes – for example, by introducing:
   a) competence frameworks
   b) job specifications
   c) role and person profiles
   d) selection and assessment centres

4. achieving an optimum balance between development and maintenance staff.

During year 2 **consolidate the core workforce and source operational personnel** – including by:

1. completing the policy of localisation

2. developing the competence of the core workforce staff – for example, by:
   a) training all staff, according to need
   b) seconding senior Chinese staff to Head Office

3. sourcing and inducting an experienced local operational management team – for example, by seconding:
   a) local managers to head office
   b) suitable managers from head office (including retired)

4. being ready to appoint entry-level and semi-skilled operational staff – for example, by: developing appropriate recruitment and training plans for entry-level and semi-skilled operational staff – such as, by identifying:
   – potential job candidates
   – the contents and sources of suitable initial training programmes

During year 3, **appoint operational staff** – including by implementing recruitment and training plans for entry-level and semi-skilled operational staff.

RECRUITMENT AND SELECTION
State employment agencies
Depending on their legal status, some foreign employers may not be allowed to employ Chinese staff directly, but be required to hire them through a state employment agency, such as the **Foreign Enterprise Service Corporation** (FESCO).

Not all offices of such agencies follow standard terms of business or even a single practice, so that it is possible for employees of the same foreign company in – for example – Beijing, Shanghai and Guangzhou to be hired on different terms.

Wherever possible, given the choice, you should opt to pay employees directly rather than via the agency – since, in this way, they are:

♦ not only guaranteed to receive their agreed wage in full

♦ but also more likely to feel part of your workforce – rather than still being technically employed by the agency – and, thus, better motivated.

Whichever option you choose, the agency will still require a monthly fee and contributions to its various welfare schemes – such as: pension and unemployment; and accident, sickness and medical insurance.

For each employee, the agency will hold their official personnel file (*dàng'àn*). When they first move from an SOE to a foreign employer, the agency must negotiate their release, and recover that file, from the SOE – until when they are technically not at liberty to join the foreign company.

Recruitment
Rather than recruit staff through the government employment agencies, who may only send you whom they wish, I recommend using traditional Western methods that will give you a wider and freer choice of applicant – including international recruitment consultants and 'head-hunters' represented in China.

Selection

Selecting Chinese staff suitable to work in a foreign company is a daunting task, especially if they have never done so before.

Thus, having successfully built from virtually scratch a small mainland Chinese workforce to work alongside a few UK and Hong Kong colleagues, I suggest the following guidelines for selecting staff:

Do...

◆ favour those who have previously worked for a foreign employer and/or been abroad – to avoid problems of the employee being released by the SOE, as explained above.

For example:

1. My PA was branded a 'traitor' by her previous Chinese employer.
2. Another employee was recalled by his previous Chinese employer.

In both cases, they came from relatively privileged families: perhaps it was because the latter's father was an ambassador that he felt obliged to toe the line.

Not to mention that they should adapt more easily to your business culture.

◆ use **competence-based selection procedures** and **assessment centres** based on specific **job descriptions** or **role profiles**; and do not shirk from including **practical skills tests**. In other words: start as you mean to go on, by using Western HRM techniques (but adapted for China) from the beginning. This will not only deter the mere 'job seekers' and weed out the incompetent, but also attract the competent who will relish the challenge. For example, in this way I retained the interest of a new Chief Representative whose appointment could not be confirmed for several months (due to my employer's international restructuring).

+ ask **controversial questions** at interview; and appoint those who argue with you – as mentioned earlier: China is full of 'yes (wo)men' with no initiative. The following examples illustrate this:
  1. One reason I chose my PA was that, after taking her to lunch so that my wife could interview her too, she said that she did not like the food.
  2. If the Office Manager had not had the confidence to challenge me at interview, she might have lacked the courage to report a suspected – but never proven – fraud.

+ use **probing questions**, and be prepared to follow lines of enquiry even where you feel uncomfortable. As an example: had I not done so, I might have appointed as a marketeer and market researcher an ex-PLA intelligence officer who – eventually – confessed that she would resort to unprintable tactics to promote the business.

+ follow the eighth of Jiang Zemin's Eight Dos and Don'ts:
  – 'Appoint people on their merits; do not resort to malpractice in personnel placement'.

Do not...
+ rely on, or be 'bullied' into following, the very Chinese favoured practice of **personal recommendation**

+ allow yourself to be pressured by your JV partner to foist on you more staff than the business actually requires – since invariably they will be ex-SOE and, hence, espouse poor SOE practices.

+ indulge in **nepotism**.

Job descriptions

Job descriptions will help not only recruitment, but also job evaluation and reward, as indicated above and below respectively.

They do not need to be lengthy or complicated, such as found in the West. For the junior roles, it is quite sufficient to limit them to key performance indicators (KPIs) or accountabilities, so that the job holder knows what to do and the standard required.

EXAMPLES

1. Office Secretary
- secretarial duties, including: answering telephone calls, typing, handling incoming and out-going mail, and similar
- liaising with the: relevant authorities to renew the office registration; landlord to pay office rental and public utilities bills; and approved suppliers to repair and maintain the office equipment, machinery and furniture
- purchase and stock-control of stationery
- booking travel and hotels
- keep the petty cash and bank account books in accordance with the company's international accounting procedures.

2. Driver
- drive the boss safely and on time
- ensure that the boss's car is in sound mechanical condition and clean.

In this way, any subsequent confrontations – for example: about poor performance or levels of pay – should have a focus that, whilst not wholly 'face saving', may help employer and employee reach a mutual understanding of each other's position and thereby maintain harmony.

Names

Whilst at school or university, many Chinese take Western first names that sound like their own given name – such as 'Vivian' for 'Huainan' and 'Pauline' for 'Yuping' – but not all.

Do not be surprised, therefore, if you are asked – like plantation owners of old – to 'name' members of your Chinese workforce; and be prepared to steer them away from the more unusual names.

EXAMPLES

1. My first driver was named 'Henry' – but only because a colleague in a similar foreign company was already called 'James'!
2. One of my staff who chose the name 'Hubert' was persuaded by a colleague to call himself 'Mark' instead.

Staff who do not wish to adopt Western first-names should not be prevailed upon to do so. As in other cultures, a Chinese person's name and identity are closely intertwined, so that to change the former is to threaten the latter.

EXAMPLES

1. My second driver was always called by his family name 'Xue', which did not have the same sense of inferiority as may prevail in other countries.
2. One of my female colleagues was also addressed by her family name 'Song' because of its lyrical connotations.

What you are called is down to you: I opted for my first name, rather than *laoban* (although I was affectionately called that, even by my expatriate colleagues), or Sir, Director or Mr So-and so.

COMPENSATION AND BENEFITS

In SOEs, **pay** has been notoriously low, but topped up by the iron rice bowl.

It is not surprising, therefore, that many Chinese choose to work for foreign employers, attracted by the prospect of higher wages.

EXAMPLE

In 1997, those ex-SOE staff whom I recruited probably trebled their take-home pay.

However, pay may be irrational, still determined by age and influence rather than performance.

Job evaluation

One method of rationalising pay structures – as I did – is to introduce **job evaluation** (JE) (also known as role analysis) and **performance appraisal/management/review**, using a tried-and-tested methodology.

EXAMPLE

I have used the HAY-MSL JE system as a tool to develop the following table purely to suggest the relativity between job-sizes, expressed as notional

Evaluated Units (EUs) – *not* to determine the size *per se* of each job – and consequently an equitable pay-scale by reference to the most senior.

Job title	EUs	Base pay
Chief representative	631	100
Administration manager	417	49
Confidential bilingual PA	252	32
IT analyst-programmer	298	35
Office secretary	178	17
Driver	097	15

Note: the driver's base pay appears disproportionate for two reasons – his:

1. Daily working hours are based on those of his boss plus travel time between the latter's home and the office.

2. Base pay includes regular overtime and weekend working.

However, this approach requires great sensitivity to the considerations of 'face' and hierarchism. Even Chinese colleagues who have studied at an overseas post-graduate business school may have difficulty accepting as practice what they have only encountered in theory.

Equal opportunities
As well as equality of the sexes, the Chinese Constitution of 1982 also espouses the principle of **equal pay for work of equal value**.

Allowances
To compensate for the loss of the 'iron rice bowl' perks, it is not uncommon to pay **allowances** on top of base salaries – sometimes for a whole range of benefits, such as: travel, meals, tax, additional personal accident and/or medical insurance, clothing etc.

I recommend:

♦ Rolling up all such allowances into base pay, in particular those that are intrinsic to a role and/or common to all or most staff – which should: not only simplify matters for employer and employee alike; but also, by effectively hiding the same, discourage staff from making comparisons and thereby infer a ranking system, albeit artificial, so dear to their hearts.

♦ Maintaining as separate genuine allowances those that are a function of seniority, special skill or cost-of-living, expressed as a percentage of base pay.

EXAMPLE		
Job holder	**Allowance**	**Say**
Chief representative	Housing allowance	17.5%
Administration manager		
Confidential bilingual PA	Language allowance	15%
IT analyst-programmer	District allowance	Beijing 12.5% Shanghai 7.5%
Office secretary		
Driver		

Income tax
Given the choice between who is responsible for tax: employer or employee – opt for the latter!

Holidays
In China, you may find any of the following three situations:

1. Employers may grant holiday entitlement (and not much at that) in arrears only – that is: an employee has to earn paid leave in advance, and is not allowed to take any until they have completed a qualifying period, often the first year.

2. Staff who leave mid-term may have to forfeit their total entitlement for the current holiday year – that is: there is no pro-rata provision.

3. All employees may enjoy the same entitlement, irrespective of seniority and length of service.

However, I do not favour staff working for solid periods of one year followed by a single annual leave; but recommend:

- Adopting a pro-rata system based on trust, regulated through the wage roll – that is: staff may take leave at their and operational convenience; and any days 'owed' to the company or them on resignation are recovered by deducting pay or compensated by payment in lieu, respectively.

- Introducing a sliding scale of annual leave according to length of service as a means of rewarding loyalty.

STAFF MANAGEMENT AND DEVELOPMENT

Reviewing and reprimanding staff

Reviewing and reprimanding Chinese staff can be a 'face' minefield – for example, to:

- leave Chinese staff in no doubt as to their inadequate performance or inappropriate behaviour

- gain their agreement to (their need to) improve

- allow them to 'walk tall' as if they were the employee of the month

require not only well-honed interpersonal and HRM skills but also a wide range of synonyms, in an effort to save 'face'.

Whilst using an intermediary is an acceptable and accepted **conflict management** tool in China, at some stage you need to deal with recalcitrant staff face-to-face.

When – or rather before – that day arrives, you should at least seek advice and guidance from a competent Chinese colleague.

Additionally, you might consider asking your colleague to be present at the disciplinary meeting, to guide you and ensure 'fair play' for the employee concerned – but without causing the latter a further loss of 'face' by remonstrating with them in front of another.

As a foreigner, you can – as I successfully did – plead each party's insufficient command of the other's language to explain the presence of your advisor as an 'interpreter'.

Performance management

One method of countering poor performance, and improving existing and developing new skills that may avoid or reduce issues of 'face' is to use a performance management system that focuses on future challenges and developments rather than past misdemeanours and shortcomings.

EXAMPLE

Confidential Bi-Lingual PA

Last year's achievements

In the last 12 months, you have made significant progress in the transition from a Chinese SOE to a Western company and the acquisition and exercise of new skills.

In the process, you have vindicated my confidence in your language skills (example); and gained a reputation at head office for helpfulness towards overseas visitors. Well done!

Recently, you have started to exercise greater objectivity (example) and take a Western view of business issues, even sometimes criticising Chinese business practice (example). Also, unlike some Chinese colleagues, you are no longer afraid to admit errors and accept criticism. Thank you!

Next year's objectives

During the next 12 months, please concentrate on developing the following aspects of your job:

1. Interpretation and translation
    a) Translate more idiomatically than literally (example)
    b) Interpret more objectively (example).

2. Personal assistance
    a) Take greater initiative and act with greater freedom on my behalf, within your agreed areas of competence and authority (examples)
    b) Anticipate my needs, by offering help or asking for work rather than waiting for me to approach you
    c) Induct my family into Chinese culture and way of life.

Next year's personal development

To achieve your objectives, I propose the following specific development actions for you, as well as normal on-going on-the-job training:

1. Interpretation and translation
   a) Advanced language training at the ABC Institute
   b) Coaching from so-and-so, an experienced Chinese Government interpreter
   c) Coaching from me in English, as a fellow-linguist.

2. Personal assistance
   a) Personal Skills Course at the XYZ Institute
   b) Appropriate basic training in meeting skills, assertiveness and business English
   c) Coaching from me and so-and-so's PA.

This may sound like so much pie in the sky: but it did bring my Chinese bilingual PA the accolade of being named Secretary of the Year by the *China Daily*.

Skills training

Given their education system, Chinese staff are likely to have excellent technical theoretical knowledge and practical skills, but little if any competence in **management techniques** and **interpersonal skills** – for which reason you should be prepared to invest in training them accordingly.

Graduates should speak some **English** – which is a compulsory component of many degrees – or other **foreign language**. However, you should not make any assumptions about their proficiency, not even those who are language graduates, because – unlike their Western counterparts – they may have never:

♦ been taught and/or examined by native speakers
♦ visited the target country
♦ been assessed orally

particularly if they were educated under Mao.

Accordingly, you should expect to have to invest in improving their **language skills**.

How you train is down to you. However, whichever method you choose, you should be aware:

♦ that (according to Global Excellence at <u>www.globalexcellence.com</u>) Chinese trainees may exhibit the following classroom behaviour:

1. 'People on courses, unless they are from the older generation, expect and want to participate.'

2. 'They are sensitive about "face", though, and do not want to be embarrassed in public.'

3. 'Participants may hesitate to "show off" their knowledge or expertise as humility is considered a positive trait.'

♦ of the following differences between:

Training outcomes in China versus the West		
Where	What happens	Outcome
West	staff are expected not only to apply new learning in the workplace but also to share it with colleagues	by training one you train many, which is a cost effective method of staff development
China	**'knowledge is power'** – that is: it serves the advancement of the individual over their colleagues	to share new learning dilutes that power, which in turn weakens personal advancement

So, if you expect your Chinese protégés, returning from the West with the MBAs you sponsored, to feel obliged to 'pay you back' by sharing their new-found knowledge with others, you could be in for a bitter disappointment.

Inter-cultural training

Finally, you will, of course, need to train staff in **inter-cultural issues** – both Chinese and expatriate – starting with yourself!

As regards the latter, up-to-date research by Hong Kong Baptist University (*BRC Papers on Cross-Cultural Management*) reached the the following conclusions:

1. 'Expatriate managers who have received training adjust more quickly in their assignments and are more satisfied with these assignments than those who have not received any training.'

2. 'On the other hand, there was unexpectedly no relationship between training and how successful the managers were in their assignments.'

3. 'Those who had received sequential training were more satisfied with their assignments than those who did not receive any training at all.'

Inter-cultural training comes in many shapes and sizes, from reading a cheap book to a residential week-long course in China costing a small fortune.

What constitutes the ideal course will depend on each person's particular requirements and any relevant experience (such as: previous overseas business dealings, foreign travel or study periods abroad).

Thus, it would be invidious for me to make any recommendations, except to mention the tailor-made China-specific business briefings offered in the UK by **Farnham Castle** – to which, as stated in the Introduction, my contributions form the basis of this book. (For further details, see: Appendix 10.1.)

Meanwhile, I never cease to be amazed by how little time and money international companies are willing to spend on preparing their staff to work with the Chinese, whilst at the same time pouring vast amounts of money into China.

Saving a few days or pounds or dollars out of a long-term multi-million pound or dollar project is:

- at best: a false economy
- at worst: to spoil the ship for a halfpennyworth of tar and may prejudice the outcome.

Whereas to invest such time or money may benefit the venture by:

- if not: doing things right
- at least: not doing things wrong.

For **Joint Ventures**, inter-cultural (management) training is critical to success through each partner thoroughly understanding the other.

Staff retention
Training should aid **staff retention** by: sending out a message of long-term commitment to your local workforce; and thereby engendering reciprocal loyalty amongst a new generation of young Chinese managers keen to develop new, shortage and, hence, marketable skills – who might otherwise be tempted to sell themselves to the highest bidder.

Promotion
Promotion is another brain-teaser for the Chinese. Traditionally a function of age in the footprints of dead men's shoes, you may now find it easier to promote on merit, by having recourse to the eighth of Jiang Zemin's Eight Dos and Don'ts:

> 'Appoint people on their merits; do not resort to malpractice in personnel placement.'

EXAMPLE

In 1998 a very senior Chinese government official – involved in the restructuring of SOEs – asked me what to do with six bright graduates, all worthy of promotion, when there was only one vacancy available? My answer was simple and twofold:

1. Assess them all, and promote the most able one on merit alone.

2. The question should have been: 'How to motivate and retain the remaining five?'

Disciplining and dismissing staff
Fortunately for you (but not for the staff!) Chinese **employment law** does not protect employees to the same extent as in the West.

Thus, from a legal stance, disciplining and dismissing staff is probably less legally fraught than in your home country.

However, this is no excuse for cavalier or callous HRM – unless you wish to lose the goodwill of the local business community which, thanks to your employees' *guanxi* grapevine, will seek to discredit you, whether or not you were in the right.

HELPFUL HINTS

HRM function

At the risk of stating the obvious, you should:

- appoint a senior Chinese colleague to have specific accountability for HRM (solely or as part of a wider function)

- develop transparent HRM policies and practices; and make copies available to all the staff.

However, research by Cornell University (*Working Paper 98–31*) indicates that this may not always be wholly effective in China for the following three possible reasons:

1. 'Government intervention may limit HR departments' ability to act strategically.'

2. 'HR departments may not have enough power to act strategically.'

3. 'HR departments may have few capabilities to respond to line executives' demands.'

Loose cannons

It is not unreasonable to expect Chinese staff who choose to work for a foreign employer to abide by the values and practices of that employer.

Despite your best efforts, perhaps following some of the foregoing advice, you may still find that you have a loose cannon or maverick in your midst.

If you have no alternative but to 'let them go', ensure you have a damage limitation strategy to mitigate the *guanxi* backlash alluded to above.

Everyone needs a Vivian

Throughout the book, I have made constant reference to my Chinese bilingual PA...Vivian.

It will not come as a surprise, therefore, to learn that, as a result of, and in response to, the many practical questions during my briefings at Farnham Castle, my clients and I have come to the conclusion that 'everybody needs a Vivian' – with the brief to:

- Help the expatriate boss operate at a personal and professional level as efficiently and effectively as possible as if he were bilingual Chinese-English and fully conversant with living and working in China.

- Translate idiomatically and interpret objectively for the boss.

- Act as confidential PA and confidante to the boss – including: arranging travel, appointments, permits and other work-related personal and personnel issues.

- Supervise the boss's domestic staff (e.g. driver and maid).

- Support and coach the boss and family members, insofar as required by their unfamiliarity with the Chinese language, culture and mores.

CODA

And so we come full circle, and finish this book where it began – with Confucius, who was right when he said:

> 'What you do not want done to yourself, do not do to others.' (*Analects* 15:23)

Perhaps those foreigners – mentioned in the opening chapters – whose favourite pastime is 'China bashing', should ask themselves why they have problems with their Chinese workforce, colleagues and JV partners. Could it possibly have anything to do with their HRM style, totally oblivious to the influences, protocols and behaviours that underpin Chinese work practices and business ethos?

Having read this book, hopefully you will not make the same mistake; but be able, as the sub-title suggests, to work more effectively with Chinese cultures.

Appendices

APPENDIX 1.1 – HISTORICAL CONTEXT OF CONFUCIUS

When (BC)	Where	What
578	Rome	Servius Tullius becomes king; and organises Rome as a soldier state, classifying citizens by wealth as the basis for taxation and military rank
566	India	Birth of **The Buddha**
551	China	**Birth of Confucius**
	Britain	Celts from Europe arrive in Britain (mainly Ireland, but also England and Scotland)
550	Rome	Servius Tullius allies Rome with her neighbours as the **Latin League**. At home, he reputedly gives limited power to the plebeian assembly
540	Persia	The Persians defeat and replace the Babylonian Empire
539		The Persians liberate Jerusalem and allow the Israelites exiled in Babylon to return home
534	Rome	Tarquinius Superbus becomes the last king; kills many senators; and revokes the plebeians' concessions
520		Tarquinius uses cunning, military supremacy and diplomatic marriage to establish Rome as the undisputed head of the Latin League

509	Rome	Founding of the **Roman Republic**. (According to tradition, Tarquinius was dethroned following the **rape of Lucretia** by his son)
507		The Etruscans besiege (and probably capture and briefly occupy) Rome
500?–400?		Rome and her allies are constantly at war with the Etruscans in the north and the mountain tribes to the south
500?	Mexico	Monte Albán is founded, and becomes the centre of Zapotec culture
496	Greece	Birth of **Sophocles** (philosopher)
490		**Battle of Marathon**
484?		Birth of **Euripides** (playwright)
		The Spartans repel the Persians at **Thermopylae**. Wiped out, their bravery becomes almost legendary
480	Britain	Large numbers of Celts arrive in Britain, significantly altering the make-up of Britain's population, and heralding Britain's **Iron Age** culture
479	China	**Death of Confucius**
475–425?	Greece	Athens reaches her political and cultural pinnacle (as exemplified by the works of **Aeschylus**, **Aristophanes**, **Euripides** and **Sophocles**), becoming a major commercial centre on the eastern Mediterranean
472		Birth of **Socrates** (philosopher)

APPENDIX 1.2 – DEVELOPMENT OF CONFUCIANSIM

When	What
Classical Period of Chinese Philosophy	
551 BC	**Birth of Confucius**
Han Dynasty 206 BC to 220 AD	Confucius' works are taught in academic institutions and underpin the subsequent entrance requirements of the cvil service – where preferment depends on knowledge of the Chinese classics In this way, Confucianism dominates political and intellectual life
Neo-Taoist and Buddhist period	
Between times	Although challenged and temporarily eclipsed by **Taoism** and **Buddhism**, the Confucian Classics remain scholars' staple instructional diet
Tang Dynasty 618 AD to 907 AD	Confucianism is encouraged; and, since Confucian students' scholarship ensures them political advancement, gradually re-emerges stronger than before as the state orthodoxy
Neo-Confucian period	
Between times	Confucianism becomes adulterated with Taoist and Buddhist ideas
Qing Dynasty 1644 AD to 1911 AD	Confucianism is purified, reverting to its Han Dynasty form; while scholars re-inforce the study of the Confucian texts with philology, history and archaeology
Modern Period	
Republic 1911 AD to 1949 AD	Confucianism falls from grace as being decadent and reactionary; and loses its traditional pillars of imperial and family structures and systems. As a result (unlike when challenged on previous occasions) Confucianism is confronted with more social turbulence than it can adjust to. Replaced by Western systems
People's Republic 1949 onwards	Confucianism is further relegated, with the demotion of family structures and systems, and the discouragement of the Confucian classics; and thus no longer dominates political life and institutions. Replaced by **Marxism** (Leninism then Maoism)
The future	Some scholars believe that Confucianism has proved itself robust enough in the past to remain the bedrock of Chinese ethics in the future

APPENDIX 2.1 – CHRONOLOGY OF THE OPIUM WARS

When	What
1760	The British East India Company had started trading in Guangzhou for porcelain, silk and especially tea, her thirst for which created a huge balance of payments in favour of the Chinese, who were willing exporters but disdained importing Western goods
1793	Britain's attempt to establish a trade treaty with China was rejected by the Chinese Emperor on the grounds that Western and other 'barbarians' could never have equality with the Celestial Empire (an allusion to the Confucian elevation of the Chinese Emperor to the status of the Son of Heaven)
	To restore the balance of trade, the British East India Company began smuggling into China cheap Indian opium (a drug only the very wealthy Chinese could afford until now)
1820	As a result, the number of opium addicts amongst ordinary Chinese escalated to such an extent that China's trade surplus became a deficit
1836	The Chinese Emperor outlawed the opium trade; ordered the punishment of dealers and users; and even appealed to the British Queen to end the traffic. But all to no avail
1839 to 1842	In another attempt to enforce the ban, the Chinese authorities seized and burned chests of opium in Guangzhou Consequently, the British retaliated by: ♦ waging the **First Opium War** ♦ forcing the Chinese to open their doors to foreign trade (giving rise to the expression '**gunboat diplomacy**') ♦ imposing on China the **Treaty of Nanjing**, as a means of exacting the trade preferences Britain sought
	During the next two years France and the USA extracted similar treaties

1856 to 1860	As China's observance of the Treaty's terms for the expansion of trade fell far short of the Western powers' expectations, Britain and France soon found an excuse to renew hostilities During the **Second Opium War**, new treaties (known collectively as the **Treaty of Tianjin**) were signed, further favouring the West However, the Chinese Emperor refused to ratify the treaty. Consequently, a joint Anglo-French expeditionary force: – **invaded** the Chinese capital (Beijing) – **destroyed** the Imperial Summer Palace (allegedly in retaliation for Chinese atrocities to Western prisoners) – **enforced** the ratification of earlier treaties by enacting the **Beijing Conventions**

APPENDIX 2.2 – TERMS OF THE UNEQUAL TREATIES

The treaties that the Chinese were forced to sign by the Western powers during and at the end of the Opium Wars – known in China collectively as **The Unequal Treaties** – and observe for the next 100 years (until 1943) forcibly and unfairly:

♦ opened **Shanghai** and four other **Treaty Ports** (known as '**concessions**') to foreign trade and residents

♦ ceded **Hong Kong** and **Kowloon** to Great Britain

♦ granted **extra-territoriality** to foreign nationals of the Treaty Powers resident in China – by which they were:
 – subject to the laws of their homeland only, not of China
 – tried by their own judges or at their consulates

♦ included a **most-favoured-nation clause**, whereby any privilege that China granted to one Treaty Power automatically applied to all Treaty Powers – which practice eventually spawned a network of foreign control over the entire Chinese economy

♦ capped the **import-duty** into China at 5%, to stop the Chinese arbitrarily imposing excessive duties – which practice denied China sufficient import duties to protect domestic markets and promote economic modernisation

♦ enforced the presence of **foreign gunboats** on the rivers and coasts of China

APPENDIX 2.3 – 15TH AND 16TH CENTURY NAVIGATORS

Zheng He	
Nationality	Chinese
Number of voyages	7
Dates of voyages	1405 – 1433
Number of ships	41 – 317
Number of men	27,500 – 30,000
Claim to fame	Led the world's earliest extensive naval expeditions, visiting 37 countries from Vietnam to East Africa

Christopher Columbus	
Nationality	Italian-born, sailed for Spain
Number of voyages	4
Dates of voyages	1492 – 1504
Number of ships	3 – 17
Number of men	104 – 1,200
Claim to fame	First European to explore the Americas since a largely forgotten Viking foray 400 years earlier

Vasco da Gama	
Nationality	Portuguese
Number of voyages	3
Dates of voyages	1497 – 1524
Number of ships	4 – 14
Number of men	n/a
Claim to fame	Discovered the sea route from Europe to India, by rounding Africa's Cape of Good Hope

Ferdinand Magellan	
Nationality	Portuguese-born, sailed for Spain
Number of voyages	1
Dates of voyages	1519 – 1522
Number of ships	5
Number of men	270
Claim to fame	Led the first circumnavigation of the globe. He was killed in the Philippines, but one ship made it back to Spain

Francis Drake	
Nationality	English
Number of voyages	9
Dates of voyages	1567 – 1596
Number of ships	2 – 30
Number of men	166
Claim to Fame	When not battling Spain, Drake led the second global circumnavigation and explored the west coast of North America and the Pacific

Source: www.time.com/time/asia

APPENDIX 4.1 – OTHER GIFTS I RECEIVED

Received		From	Occasion
Tablecloth		Ministry of Foreign Trade and Economic Cooperation	Delivering seminar on human resource management
Key ring	with logo	Foreign insurance companies	Banquet to celebrate opening of representative offices
Luggage label			
Pocket telescope			
Framed/mounted paper money		HSBC	Opening of new office
		EU Embassy	Launch of Euro
Commemorative coins and medals		Beijing Finance College	Tenth anniversary celebration
		Jiang Zemin's brother-in-law	Visit to London
Chopsticks (silver)		China Club, Beijing	Wedding anniversary
Book (illustrated)		Personal Assistant	
CD		British Chamber of Commerce	Banquet for British Prime Minister
		Colleague	Welcome to China
Coffee table		Personal Assistant	House warming
Kite			Easter
Calendar		Colleague	Lunch at home
Plant for desk		Colleague	Office move
Conference folder and pen (with logo)		China-Britain Business Council	Attending investment conference
Coffee service and Vase		All colleagues	Farewell
Book (illustrated)		Colleague	
Tea pot		Colleague's wife	
Tea service		Driver	
Table cloth (handmade)		Maid	
Antique ink pot		Personal Assistant	
Stamp album with mounted stamps and first day covers		Two colleagues	
Cloisonné pots		Chinese teacher	
Commemorative plate		Beijing Finance College	
Commemorative medals		People's Insurance Company Shanghai Finance College	

APPENDIX 9.1. – SUPPORT SERVICES

It would be invidious for me to try to list all the support services available to foreign business(wo)men since there are so many that inevitably some services and/or home countries might be inadvertently overlooked and thus omitted.

Moreover, merely listing such services does not necessarily indicate or guarantee their usefulness.

Rather, I suggest that you contact:

◆ in general: the commercial section of the Chinese Embassy in your home country and of your home Embassy in China

◆ in particular: organisations whose web sites are listed in the Bibliography

and, from personal experience, I can recommend the following organisations, quoted in the body of this book:

◆ **Farnham Castle International Briefing and Conference Centre** at: www.farnhamcastle.com

◆ **Apco China** at: www.apcoworldwide.com/Asia/contact.html

APPENDIX 10.1 – FARNHAM CASTLE CHINA BRIEFING

Typical session outlines
Where am I going? – the country today

Looking at your new environment – the key issues that shape the country today

♦ **The place** – location, geography, climate

♦ **The politics** – the government, key personalities, macro economics, local and international relationships

♦ **The people** – ethnicity, culture, religions, topical issues

How should I behave?

Cultural sensitivity – the impact of local culture on everyday life

♦ **Understanding attitudes and values**

♦ **Social etiquette: saying and doing the right thing** – hospitality, traditions, gifts

♦ **Use of language** – communication styles, simple greetings, formal and informal styles

♦ **Use of humour: is it really funny**? – the local sense of humour, examples

♦ **Words are not enough: understanding gestures and body language** – interpreting gestures and body language, personal space

Getting down to business

An insight into understanding how business really works

♦ **How we do things around here** – business customs and ethics

♦ **Who's in charge?** – power structures and hierarchies

♦ **The importance of networking** – and how its done

♦ **Business etiquette** – dos and don'ts

♦ **Women in business** – status and protocol

- **Running a meeting** – chairing, seating, purpose, conduct
- **Dress codes** – formal, informal, social and business
- **Effective negotiation and communication** – the right communication style
- **Business or pleasure?** – business entertaining, how it's done and who pays the bill!
- **The local business scene** – chambers of commerce, rotary etc, local points of contact
- **Hints and tips** – support services, communications, transport

Bibliography

LUCKY EIGHT

I acknowledge and recommend the following eight sources of information on doing business with the Chinese, each one unique and different from the rest in content and/or perspective (in alphabetical order):

Beyond the Chinese Face: Insights from Psychology, Michael Harris Bond, Oxford University Press (China), Hong Kong, 1991 (125 pages). Especially useful for serious students of the Chinese psyche interested in understanding how the Chinese think and behave in society and at work, this book is an indispensable guide to many of their underpinning behaviours in general, and 'face' in particular.

China Business Handbook, *China Economic Review*, Alain Charles Publishing Ltd, London (387 pages). Updated and issued annually by the publishers of the *China Economic Review*, this book not only summarises Chinese business practices and issues but also provides an overview of each region. Particularly valuable are the useful contacts listed under the Business Associations, Business Directory, Government Ministries and Internet Contact Guide.

Culture Shock! China, Kevin Sinclair with Iris Wong Po-yee, Kuperard, London, 3rd edition, 1999 (317 pages). Anyone familiar with the *Culture Shock!* series will not be disappointed by its China companion. Significantly revised and enlarged in 1999 by its journalist authors (one Western, the other Chinese), the book is not only virtually up-to-date but also (as you would expect from newspaper professionals) a jolly good read, full of colourful and relevant detail. Although only one chapter albeit substantial is specifically aimed at business(wo)men, it contains much useful and relevant background information. Finally: to make sure you learn the lessons, the book finishes with a 'Cultural Quiz'!

Dealing with the Chinese, Scott D. Seligman, Management Books 2000, UK, 1997 (192 pages). Revised and reissued as: *Chinese Business Etiquette*, Scott D. Seligman, Warner Books, USA, 1999 (281 pages). First published in 1990 and revised a decade later, this book lives up to its sub-title originally of *A Practical Guide to Business Etiquette* and later *A Guide to Protocol, Manners and Culture in the PRC*. Based on Seligman's experience of advising US companies entering China, it offers very detailed advice and rules for conducting business relations with the Chinese. Of particular help are the bulleted summaries at the end of each chapter, such as: 'Eleven Points on Cultural Differences' or 'Nine Tips for Foreigners in China'. If only for the chapter on 'Negotiating with the Chinese' in its original but not revised edition the book is a *tour de force*.

Encountering the Chinese, Hu Wenzhong and Cornelius L Grove, Intercultural Press, USA, 1991 (192 pages). Published in the early 1990s and sub-titled *A Guide for Americans*, much of this book is still relevant today and to other foreigners. Providing detailed guidance on how to interact with the Chinese, it benefits from combining both a Chinese and Western perspective, and comparing/contrasting them, having been written by an American cross-culturalist and a Chinese academic. Worthy of special mention are the many footnotes, offering even more exhaustive guidance, but without interrupting the prime focus.

Negotiating China: Case Studies and Strategies, Carolyn Blackman, Allan & Unwin, Australia, 1997 (205 pages). Published in 1997 and drawing on evidence and experience going back over at least the previous two decades, the lessons learnt and consequent advice given are just as valuable today as then. After a general overview of the framework within which Chinese negotiators operate, and a detailed exposé of their tactics, the second half of the book comprises six comprehensive case studies that illustrate and put into context such framework and tactics. Particularly useful are: the quotations from Chinese textbooks on how to negotiate with foreigners; and, for the hard-pressed jet-setting Westerner, rushing from one deal and country to the next, a 'Quick Reference Chart to Chinese Negotiating Characteristics'. One of the few overseas-published business books on sale at the Foreign Languages Bookshop, Shanghai, Spring 2003.

Turning Bricks into Jade: Critical Incidents for Mutual Understanding among Chinese and Americans, Mary Margaret Wang, Richard W. Brislin, Wei-zhong Wang, David Williams, Julie Haiyan Chao, Intercultural Press, USA, 2000 (234 pages). Despite its sub-title, this book is relevant to foreigners other than Americans. Consisting of 41 mini case-studies ('critical incidents'), for each one you are: first confronted with a 'culture clash' between its Western and Chinese protagonists; then asked to choose from a number of solutions; and finally presented with a commentary on each choice – whose appropriateness varies, rather than being either just a right or wrong answer. Experiential in style, therefore, the book may be used as a cultural training manual for individual study or group learning.

Xenophobe's Guide to the Chinese, J C Yang, Oval Books, 3rd edition, London, 1999 (64 pages). Describing itself as 'an irreverent look at the beliefs and foibles' of the Chinese, this slim, incisive volume offers brief, no-nonsense perceptions acquired over 40 years in such an amusing manner that you will not be able to put it down but read it at one go from cover-to-cover in under two hours.

BUSINESS GUIDES

The following sources of information deal primarily with doing business with the Chinese:

CBBC China Guide, China-Britain Business Council, www.cbbc.org/china-guide/index.com. 2003

China Briefing, China Strategic Ltd and Dezan Shira & Associates Ltd, Shanghai, monthly.
Further information: www.china-briefing.com.

China-Britain Trade Review, China-Britain Business Council, London, monthly. Further information: www.cbbc.org.

China Business and Travel Guide 2002/3, China Knowledge Press, Singapore, 2002.

China Business Guide, Robin Porter and Mandi Robinson, Keele China Business Centre and China Britain Trade Group, Ryburn Publishing, Keele University Press (UK), 1994.

China Cultural and Language Briefing, Andrew M. Williamson in: *Export Buyers Guide*, 5th edition, UK, 2002.

China Economic Review, Alain Charles Publishing Ltd, London, monthly. Further information: www.chinaeconomicreview.com.

China International Business, International Business Daily, Beijing, monthly. Further information: www.cib-online.net.

Chinese Business Etiquette and Culture, Kevin Bucknall, Boson Books, USA, 2002. An excellent book, of the same calibre as Scott D. Seligman's, and with 30% devoted to negotiations, its inclusion here rather than under the Lucky Eight is purely a reflection of my greater familiarity with the latter, published several years earlier, when trying to choose between them.

Country Commercial Guide: China, US Commercial Service, US Dept. of Commerce, www.usatrade.gov, 2002.

Culture Shock! Success to Maximise Business in China, Larry T L Luah, Time Books International, Singapore, 2001.

Doing Business in China, Tim Ambler and Morgen Witzel, Routledge, London, 2000. One of the few overseas-published business books on sale at the Foreign Languages Bookshop, Shanghai, Spring 2003.

Doing Buisness in Shanghai, China Knowledge Press Pte Ltd, Singapore, 2003. Future titles due to be pubslihed include: Beijing and Guangdong. Further information: *www.chinaknowledge.com*

Doing Business in the PRC, PricewaterhouseCoopers, USA, 1999.

Doing Business with China, Kogan Page, UK, 2000.

Living and Working in China, Employment Conditions Abroad Limited, UK, 1996.

The New Silk Road: Secrets of Business Success in China Today, John B Stuttard, John Wiley and Sons, New York, 2000.

Thinking China, Apco China, www.apcoworldwide.com, 2002.

GENERAL PUBLICATIONS

The following sources of information include useful secondary material relevant to doing business with the Chinese:

About China, China E-Travel, www.chinaetravel.com, 2002.

Asia-Inc, Praxis Communications Ltd, Hong Kong, Monthly. Further information: www.asia-inc.com.

Background Note: China, US Department of State, www.state.gov, 1997.

Beijing Review, Beijing, Weekly. Further information: www.bjreview. com.cn.

Beijing Scene Guidebook, Beijing Scene Publishing, USA, 1997.

CFO Asia, CFO Publishing Corporation, Hong Kong, Monthly. Further information: www.cfoasia.com.

China, Encarta Encyclopaedia, encarta.msn.co.uk, 2002.

China, Encyclopedia Britannica CD, De-Luxe edition, 2000.

China, Hutchinson Multimedia Encyclopedia, 2001.

China, Insight Guides, Apa Publications, 9th edition, Singapore, 2000. One of the few overseas-published travel books on sale at the Foreign Languages Bookshop, Shanghai, Spring 2003.

China, Lonely Planet Online, www.lonelyplanet.com, 2002.

China, Lonely Planet Publications, 8th edition, Australia, 2002. One of the few overseas-published travel books on sale at the Foreign Languages Bookshop, Shanghai, Spring 2003.

China ABC, Chinese Embassy, London, www.chinese-embassy.org.uk.

China Basics, China Tour, www.chinatour.com, 2002.

China Guides, Hotel Travel, www.hoteltravel.com, 2002.

China in Brief, China Internet Information Centre, www.chinagui-de.org, 2002.

China Mail, TWL Publishing (S) Pte Ltd, Singapore, quarterly. Further information: www.twlcic.com/cm.

China Today, www.chinatoday.com, 2002.

China Travel Tips, Hotel Travel, www.hoteltravel.com, 2002.

City Weekend: The Essential Guide to Modern China, City Weekend, Beijing and Shanghai, fortnightly.

Country Profile: China, Foreign Office, www.fco.gov.uk, 2002.

Cultural Essentials, China Vista, www.chinavista.com, 2002.

Far Eastern Economic Review, Review Publishing Co Ltd, Hong Kong, weekly. Further information: www.feer.com.

Simple Guide to China – Customs & Etiquette, Caroline Mason and Geoffrey Murray, Global Books Ltd, 3rd edition, UK, 1999.

Survival Facts, China E-Travel, www.chinaetravel.com, 2002.

Things Chinese, Du Feibao and Du Bai, China Travel & Tourism Press, Beijing, 2002.

Travel China Guide, www.travelchinaguide.com, 2002.

Travel Tips, China National Tourism Association, www.cnta.com, 2002.

Travel Tips, China Tour, www.chinatour.com, 2002.
Travel Tips, China Vista, www.chinavista.com, 2002.
Welcome to China, China National Tourist Office, www.cnto.org, 2002.
World Factbook: China, CIA, www.odci.gov/cia, 2002.

WEB SITES

Besides those quoted against specific business guides, general publications and specialist further reading, the following web sites – which I have scrutinised from hundreds listed on various search engines – contain useful references to doing business with the Chinese:

Business Beijing, www.cbw.com/busbj. Provides information on trade, investment and business policies in the PRC, with special emphasis on the capital. Published by the Information Office of Beijing Municipal Government, Beijing Municipal Foreign Economic and Trade Commission and Beijing Municipal Planning Commission.

China Daily Newspaper, www.chinadaily.com.cn.

China Business Desk, www.chinabusinessdesk.com. Aims to give China business news with a European dimension. In addition to global news relating to China, special attention is paid to the implications of such news from a European perspective.

Chinese Embassy USA, www.china-embassy.org/eng/index.html.

China Online, chineseculture.about.com/. Consists of hundreds of guide sites organised into 23 channels that cover more than 50,000 subjects with over 1 million links to resources on the net.

China Site, chinasite.com. Refers to China/Chinese-related web sites.

China Updates, www2.fba.nus.edu.sg/chinaupdates. Refers to China/Chinese-related sites. Developed to promote the China training programmes of the International Business Institute of the National University of Singapore Business School.

China World Consulting, www.china-w.com. Aims to provide information and assistance to the English speaking business community worldwide.

Chinese Business World, www.cbw.com/index.html.

Columbia Electronic Encyclopedia, www.infoplease.com/ipa/A0107411.html.

Economist Magazine, www.economist.com/countries/China/index.cfm

Global Edge, globaledge.msu.edu/ibrd/CountryIntro.asp?CountryI-D = 17&RegionID = 3. An outline of the business climate, political structure, history and statistical data; and directory of international business resources categorised by orientation and content.

Global Road Warrior, www.worldcell.com/wrldrw/grw/country/china/01frameset.html. Key facts and figures: business culture, advice on communication, climate, security, visas, currencies, health etc.

Great Britain China Centre, www.gbcc.org.uk. Development and management of an exchange programme with Chinese partners, and the provision of information and advice on China.

Library of Congress, www.loc.gov/rr/international/asian/china/china.html. Free online directory service for web sites: owned by Chinese businesses, organisations and individuals; sites related to China/Chinese; and sites deemed useful to the Chinese and those who deal with the Chinese.

Links to China, www.linkstochina.com

Muzi China, china.muzi.com/index1.shtml. China portal.

Near China, www.nearchina.com. Chinese news.

People Daily, english.peopledaily.com.cn/ywzd/home.html. Reference to English web sites in China.

The Beijing Page, www.beijingpage.com

Time Magazine Asia, www.time.com/time/asia

SPECIALIST FURTHER READING

In addition to the general reading listed above, I recommend the following specialised texts:

Chapter 1

Confucianism

Analects, Confucius
Quotations from: http://classics.mit.edu/ Confucius/analects.mb.txt

Confucius, Kelley L. Ross
www.friesan.com, 2002

What Confucius Thought, Megaera Lorenz
www.heptune.com, 2002

Political Environment
Quotations from Chairman Mao Tse-Tung, Foreign Languages Press, Beijing, 1966
The significance of the 15th Party Congress, Batey Burn Ltd, Hong Kong, (now Apco China) October 1997.

Political Environment and Economic Reforms
Documents of the 16th National Congress of the Communist Party of China, Foreign Languages Press, Beijing, 2002.
16th Party Congress, China Daily, www.chinadaily.com.cn, Nov. 2002.

Economic Reforms
China Special Report, Batey Burn Ltd, Hong Kong, (now Apco China) April 1998.

Open Door Policy
China in the WTO, Rio Longacre, Crown Relocations, New York, in: *Mobility*, June 2002.
Guanxi on the Web: Ten Keys to Putting the Right Face Toward China, Richard Webb, Neu Star, www.neustar.com.cn.2003
NeuStar's Guide for International Business People: The Next Frontier of Global E-Business, NeuStar, www.neustar.com.cn, 2002

Chapter 2

Geography
China, Atlapedia Online, www.atlapedia.com, 2002

History
1421: The Year China Discovered the World, Gavin Menzies, Bantam Press, London, 2002
China: A History, Arthur Cotterrell, Pimlico, London, 1995
Daily Mail Weekend Supplement, London, 9 June 2001
Traveller's History of China, Stephen Haw, Windrush Press, UK, 1995

Chapter 3

Face

The Case for Face in the Intercultural Marketplace, John Masih and David Marsh in: *Uniqueness in Unity: The Significance of Cultural Identity in European Cooperation*, Proceedings of the 5th SIETAR Europa Symposium, Prague, 1995.

Non-verbal Communication

Spontaneous Attention to Word Content Versus Emotional Tone: Differences Among Three Cultures, Keiko Ishii and Shinobu Kitayama, Kyota University, Japan; and Jose Alberto Reyes, De La Salle Univeristy, Manila, Philippines. At: www.dialogin.com, 2003.

General

East West Relationships, Sigmund Aarvik in: *Europe on the Move Fusion or Fission?*, Proceedings of the 4th SIETAR Europa Symposium, Finland, 1995.

Self-Disclosure as a therapeutic technique in Eastern and Western cultures, Nancy Bragard in: *Meeting the Intercultural Challenge: Effective Approaches in Research, Education, Training and Business*, Proceedings of the 6th SIETAR Europa Symposium, Munich, 1996.

Chapter 5

Integrating Twelve Dimensions of Negotiating Behavior and Hofestede's Work-Related Values: A Six-Country Comparison, Allan Bird, University of Missouri and Lynn Metcalf, California Polytechnic State University, USA. At: www.dialogin.com, 2003.

National Feelings on Business Negotiations: A Study in the China Context, Xinping Shi and Philip Wright, Business Research Centre, School of Business, Hong Kong Baptist University. At: The Delta Intercultural Academy, www.dialogin.com, 2003.

Non-native Speakers as Negotiators, Anne Marie Bülow-Møller in: *Crossing Borders: Communication between Cultures and Companies*, Høgskolen i Østfold, Report 2001:3, pp. 145–157, Norway, 2001. At: The Delta Intercultural Academy, www.dialogin.com, 2002.

Chapter 6

Disagreement in Authentic Chinese-British Business Meetings: Unpacking the Role of Culture, Helen Spencer-Oatey, Centre for Intercultural Training & Research, www.intercultural.org.uk, 2003.

Managing Rapport in Intercultural Business Interactions: A Comparison of Two Chinese-British Welcome Meetings, Helen Spencer-Oatey and Jianyu Xing, Centre for Intercultural Training & Research, www.intercultural.org.uk, 2003.

Both papers are excellent summaries of what can go wrong, what not to do and why!

Practical tips for speaking through an interpreter, Anthea Heffernan in: *China–Britain Trade Review*, July 2000.

Relational Management in Chinese-British Meetings, Helen Spencer-Oatey and Jianyu Xing, Centre for Intercultural Training & Research, www.intercultural.org.uk, 2003.

Silence in an Intercultural Business Meeting: Multiple Perspectives and Interpretations, Helen Spencer-Oatey and Jianyu Xing, Centre for Intercultural Training & Research, www.intercultural.org.uk, 2003. Another excellent summary of what can go wrong, what not to do and why!

Chapter 7

A Chinese Banquet, China Online, www.chineseculture.about.com, 2002.

Food, China E-Travel, www.chinaetravel.com, 2002.

Chapter 9

Product Cue Usage in Two Asian Markets: A Cross-Cultural Comparison, Sandra Forsythe and Jai Ok Kim c/o Department of Consumer Affairs, Auburn University, Alabama, USA, 2003.

Chapter 10

BRC Papers on Cross-Cultural Management: Effects of Training for China: European Expatriate Managers, Jan Selmer, Business Research Centre, School of Business, Hong Kong Baptist University at: The Delta Intercultural Academy, www.dialogin.com, 2002.

Getting Your Message Across Cultures, Richard Cook, Global Excellence, www.global-excellence.com, 2002.

Giving Feedback in a Diverse Environment, Lee Gardenswartz and Anita Rowe, www.global-excellence.com, 2002.

Line and HR Executives' Perceptions of HR Effectiveness in Firms in the PRC, Hitoshi Mitsuhashi, Hyeon Park, Patrick Wright and Rodney Chua, Center for Advanced HR Studies, Cornell University, USA, Working Paper 98–31 at: www.ilr.cornell.edu/cahrs, 2002.

Managing International Assignments, Richard Cook, Global Excellence, www.global-excellence.com, 2002.

Managing Meetings that are held in a Culturally Diverse Environment, Lee Gardenswartz and Anita Rowe, www.global-excellence.com, 2002.

Managing Multicultural Teamwork, David Trickey, TCO International Diversity Management, www.tco-international.com, 2002.

The Cross-Cultural Dimension in International Business, Richard Cook, Global Excellence, www.global-excellence.com, 2002.

They All Speak English, Don't They?, Richard Cook, Global Excellence, www.global-excellence.com, 2002.

Training Across Cultures: Facing the Global Challenge, Richard Cook, Global Excellence, www.global-excellence.com, 2002.

What's in a Name?, Richard Cook, Global Excellence, www.global-excellence.com, 2002.

Why Global Organisations Need Global Skills, Richard Cook, Global Excellence, www.global-excellence.com, 2002.

Index